HK HIKING

ADVENTUROUS HIKES
BOOK 1: HONG KONG'S NEW TERRITORIES

JAN LITTLEWOOD

Published by:

flying bottle

Conceived, written, edited and designed by: **Jan Littlewood**
All photography & image creation by: **Jan Littlewood**

Originally printed under the title:
10 Adventurous Hikes in Hong Kong's New Territories

2nd printing: **May , 2005**
Printed by:
PROjet, Hong Kong. Contact: Florence Chow, Tel. 2114 0053

HKhiking.com contact email: **books@hkhiking.com**

ISBN number: **0-9545532-2-5**

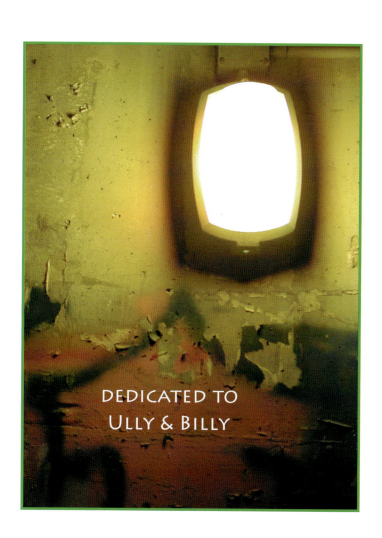

DEDICATED TO
Ully & Billy

ACKNOWLEDGEMENTS:

Spencer Cheung of Catbus Adventures (www.catbus-adventures.com), for encouraging and cultivating my interest in hiking and for being one of the most cheerful and knowledgeable hikers in Hong Kong. Thanks to Tony Tse, for encouraging me to start trailrunning, (I promise I will train more). Thanks to Libbo, for her interest and support. Finally, last, not least, thanks to Jean Yves for putting up with me babbling into a tape recorder every time we go hiking.

COMMENTS & FEEDBACK:

Please feel free to visit the website at www.hkhiking.com This will contain some basic information about the hikes in the book as well as some pictures of some of the scenery which may be encountered. This website is not guaranteed to be up to date.

Any comments, remarks or feedback are welcome. Please send them to: books@hkhiking.com

CONTENTS

THE HIKES

APPENDIX

The serene view of Plover Cove Reservoir, hike 7, as night approaches.

INTRODUCTION

1. Hong Kong's countryside & the New Territories

Many people consider Hong Kong to be the epitomy of a modern supercity, with much of the skyline being dominated by high rise buildings. But a casual glance behind the skyscrapers will reveal a lush green flora, typical of a semi-tropical climate. The proximity of Hong Kong's countryside to civilisation has the advantage that it is possible to gain quick, easy access to areas of considerable natural beauty. This leads to a variety of interesting, adventurous, fun day hikes.

The New Territories is considered by many to be the most far flung and inaccessible region of Hong Kong. This misconception has advantages, in that rural areas are often tranquil and calm, but also disadvantages, in that many people are missing out on the breathtaking beauty of Hong Kong's countryside.

The contrast between city and countryside in Hong Kong is startling and unique.

2. HKhiking.com philosophy

Our basic philosophy is to create walks that are accessible and easy to follow whilst providing interesting, unique routes. Each hike is designed to be a full and comprehensive days hike. The Adventurous Hikes series tries to add a sense of adventure to hiking in Hong Kong. Overgrown trails, steep climbs, treacherous descents and calm, hidden paths.

This does not mean that all the hikes in this book should only be attempted by the super-fit. Hikes are categorised and range from relatively user friendly to long, difficult and technically challenging. All that is assumed is a certain amount of hiking experience, the ability to use and read a map and the desire to walk along overgrown paths or steep, slippery ups and downs with a smile on your face.

3. Public transport in Hong Kong

Hong Kong is extremely well served by public transport. The MTR (Mass Transit Railway) is a mainly underground network serving Hong Kong Island, Kowloon and even reaching Lantau Island. The KCRC (Kowloon-Canton Railway Corporation), runs the East Rail, West Rail, Ma On Shan Rail and Light Rail, serving Kowloon and the New Territories. Added to this are normal buses and mini buses. There are two types of mini bus, red and green. Green buses are government run whilst red are privately run. Taxis are also numerous, readily available and cheap compared to many major cities. Red taxis serve Hong Kong Island and Kowloon, green taxis serve the New Territories and blue taxis serve Lantau Island. The appendix contains transport maps, timetables and extra information.

Taxis, KCR and a green mini bus - some of Hong Kong's excellent public transport.

4. Octopus card

The octopus card is a stored value card which can be used on all forms of public transport. Money is stored on the card at ticket offices or at 7-eleven or Ⓚ convenience stores. Once charged with money, the card is merely placed on the electronic sensors found on all forms of public transport. I recommend that you get an octopus card.

5. Accessing the hikes in this book

The starting and finishing points of all the hikes in this book can easily be accessed using public transport. This book was written with budget hikers in mind, so a taxi is always a luxurious extra as opposed to a necessity.

6. When to hike

Hong Kong has clearly defined seasons, ranging from a relatively cold and dry winter (between December and February), to a hot, humid summer (between July and September). Many people find the heat and storms in the summer particularly hard to deal with, but as long as you are well prepared (see the Hiking Hints section) and know what to expect, it is possible to hike all year round.

Overview of hikes in the book

CHINA

NORTH WEST NEW TERRITORIES

NORTH EAST NEW TERRITORIES

SAI KUNG COUNTRY PARK

CENTRAL NEW TERRITORIES

KOWLOON

HONG KONG

LAMMA

LANTAU

N

0 2 4 6 8 10km

hike 1   hike 6
hike 2   hike 7
hike 3   hike 8
hike 4   hike 9
hike 5   hike 10

<100m
101-200m
201-300m
301-400m
401-500m
501-600m
601-700m
701-800m
801-900m
>900m

USING THIS BOOK

1. Target audience

This book is aimed at hikers who are reasonably experienced and technically accomplished enough to handle almost any kind of terrain. Many of the paths described in this book are narrow, hard to find, overgrown mud paths. Descents down steep, slippery moss covered slopes and difficult, long climbs up gravelly slopes are to be expected.

2. Difficulty categories

Each of the hikes is placed in one of the following difficulty categories:

snake

Social snakes are capable of slithering up to 20km. They don't like too many hard climbs or steep, treacherous descents, but can still hold their own.

lion

Lions are brave and have no fear of difficult, technical hikes. They can keep going for up to 25km of tricky, physically challenging terrain.

kangaroo

Kangaroos can bounce along a hike for anything up to 30km, enjoying the challenge of finding paths or cascading up or down near vertical hills.

flying bottle

Reserved for hikes which are abnormally difficult technically speaking. Distance has no real bearing. Expect to have a difficult, exciting day.

3. Extra skills

One of the following extra skills may be required during a hike.

mountain goat

Mountain goats love steep, precarious, gravelly, rocky hills and never suffer from vertigo. Up or down, it makes no difference.

pathfinder

Pathfinders never get lost. No matter if the path is overgrown, difficult to find or even non existent. They will either find a path, or make one.

eel

Eels are slippery and slidey and have no worries about crossing slippery, wet river beds strewn with algae covered rocks and boulders.

4. Cover page

Each hike is preceded by a cover page which contains a wealth of information about the hike. Below is a sample cover page together with a brief description of the information contained on it.

DIFFICULTY
The estimated difficulty of the hike according to the categories on p.4.

DISTANCE
The total distance of the hike in kilometres (km).

TIME
Estimated time required to finish the hike at an average speed.

MAP
The Countryside Series map required for the hike (see p.6).

EXTRA SKILLS
Any extra skills which may be required for the hike (see p.4 for list).

START CHINESE
Starting point in Chinese characters. Useful to show taxi drivers.

START ENGLISH
Starting point in English. Useful for finding your position on a map.

GET TO START ICONS
A simple, visual description on how to get to the start using icons (see p.6).

GETTING TO START
A worded description on how to get to the start of the hike.

DESCRIPTION
A brief description of the route taken by the hike.

GET HOME ICONS
A simple, visual description on how to get home using icons (see p.6).

GETTING HOME
A worded description on how to get home after finishing the hike.

HIKE 3: Shatin round trip

summary:

20.55km   6½h   North East & Central NT

starting point: 沙田火车站

Shatin KCR station

getting to start: Shatin

Go to Shatin KCR station.

description:

The hike starts at Shatin KCR and climbs up past a temple complex, into the MacLehose trail and over Needle Hill. We then hug Shing Mun reservoir before taking a hidden path which contains an overgrown climb. You then climb a gradual hill before walking back down to Shatin KCR.

getting home: Shatin

Take the KCR from Shatin station.

WARNINGS:

Be careful of steep eroded paths near the beginning of the hike. These may be dangerous to navigate. Ignore any monkeys you might see at Shing Mun Reservoir and do not try to interact with them. Look out for eroded ravines on the mud paths towards the end of the hike.

hike Xsection:

SAMPLE COVER PAGE

XSECTION
Cross section of the hike giving an idea of the changes in altitude.

WARNINGS
Useful information on areas of the hike which require special attention.

5. Cover page icons

The icons below visually convey the information in the 'Getting to Start' and 'Getting Home' sections of the cover page.

ICON EXAMPLE	GENERAL MEANING	MEANING OF EXAMPLE
Shatin	KCR station	Shatin KCR station
Tsuen Wan	MTR station	Tsuen Wan MTR station
75K	normal bus	normal bus no. 75K
65A	green mini bus	green mini bus no.65A
$40 $40	red/green taxi	red/green taxi costing HK$40

6. Map

Simplified maps of the route are to the left of the cover page.

To the left of every cover page is a simplified map of the route you are taking. This gives you an overview of the hike and enables you to chart your progress. However, this map is NOT a substitute for the relevant Coutryside Series map of the area. Countryside Series maps are produced by the government and give excellent, detailed information, generally at a scale of 1:25 000. The map required for each hike is mentioned on the cover page. It is essential that you take this map with you, it will be of continuous use, especially if you become lost. Addresses where these maps are available are provided in Appendix, A-v.

7. Photocopying

Hong Kong can be wet, hot and humid and I don't want your book to become ruined. Please feel free to photocopy the hike you intend doing. This protects the book and also makes the description more practical to carry around.

All I ask in this respect is that you do not photocopy the hikes specifically to give them to others free of charge. As you may have guessed, this book has been written on a pretty tight budget. As such, any future titles in the series depend on financial feasibility. Please encourage others to buy their own copy if you enjoy the book and tell them not to buy it if you don't. Just be honest.

8. Main text

Below is an example of the main text in the book and a description on how the information contined in it is to be used.

DISTANCE	EXTRA INFORMATION
The numbers in the left column signify the distance in kilometres (km) from the start of each hike at which the corresponding description is found. For example: 'Continue straight ahead up the hill....' in the sample text below occurs 5.53km after the beginning of the hike. These distances are useful for orientation and calculating the distance between descriptions in the text.	Highlighted red text indicates areas of the hike where special attention may be required. There are three main headings in this category: **ATTENTION** normally occurs when you need to concentrate to find a hidden path. **TRIG. STATION** occurs when you pass a trigonometrical station on the hike. **WARNING** occurs at dangerous or technically difficult sections of the hike.

5.53 **ATTENTION** Continue straight ahead up the hill along the clear mud path at the junction, (Figure 4). Ignore the path crossing your route which is the 'Cheung Sheung Country Trail'.

Continue along the main path ignoring any major offshoots to your right or left.

Figure 4: Continue straight ahead up the hill.

6.00 **Turn right onto** the clear path leading up the hill. Do not continue straight ahead down the hill on the path you were on.

MAIN TEXT SAMPLE

BOLD TEXT	FADED TEXT	FIGURES
It should be possible to follow the hike quite easily just reading the text in bold print, saving you time. When extra information is required then read the faded text.	The faded text gives more detailed, exhaustive information and is particularly useful when lost. I have gone on the basis that too much information is better than too little.	Sometimes images are inserted into the text. These are designed to help you orientate yourself and find potentially difficult to find, hidden paths. Certainly not for aesthetic effect!

9. Appendix

The Appendix contains a wealth of information, this includes:
MTR / KCR map - to help you get to the starting point.
Bus timetables - simplified timetables for the routes used in this book.
Hike instructions - extra instructions for some of the hikes.
Useful numbers, websites & addresses - useful information for all those wishing to hike in Hong Kong.

1. Equipment list

Below is what I would subjectively consider to be the essential equipment list for anyone embarking on a hike in Hong Kong.

 WATER is the most essential item for any hiker. Always take more than you need. It could save your life.

 MAP Don't get lost. The Countryside Series maps are a must for any hike. Check your route in advance.

 FIRST AID KIT Injuries do happen, so be prepared. Take a basic first aid kit on your hikes.

 SUN CREAM Sun burn hurts and can also cause skin cancer. Never be seen without your cream.

 HAT Having the sun shining relentlessly on your head all day is a real pain. Don't forget your hat.

 BOOTS The comfort of your feet is vital whilst hiking. Always wear supportive, comfortable boots.

 FOOD There are no restaurants on the top of Sharp Peak. Always bring food with you, in case of hunger.

 TORCH Hikers regularly become lost and trapped in darkness. Never forget your torch.

 CLOTHES 2 spare T-shirts plus socks are the minimum. Jumpers are required in winter, as well as waterproofs.

 PHONE When trapped or injured a phone may be your last chance of help. At last there is a use for mobiles.

 PEOPLE Bringing someone else along is the safest and best option. At least tell someone where you'll be.

 RUCKSACK All that equipment belongs in a comfortable, adjustable, well fitting rucksack.

 STICK A stick is always useful. To support weary or damaged limbs, or even fend off monkeys and dogs.

 MONEY May come in useful, even if you can't buy your way out of trouble in the countryside.

2. Water

 I know water is mentioned above but I want to stress its importance. Water is vital in the heat and humidity of Hong Kong. In warm weather I recommend a minimum of 2 litres of water for the shortest hikes and a minimum of 4 litres for the longer hikes. None of the hikes in this book are written with the intention of purchasing water *en route*, so please carry everything you need.

3. Group size

The larger the group the slower the hike. Please consider the fact that these hikes pass through difficult, treacherous terrain. In the case of an emergency, such as a hill fire, you need to be able to shepherd yourself and the rest of your group to safety.

4. Technical issues

Many of the hikes in this book could be described as technically difficult from a hiking point of view. The secret to consistent hiking is to maintain a steady pace, rather than having fast and slow spurts. Try to relax your legs whilst going up and down hills. In particular, do not try to run down hills too quickly, this can be dangerous. Small precise steps are more controlled and efficient than huge, lunging strides. Once at the top of a hill, take a couple of deep breaths and relax your shoulders, arms and legs before continuing your hike. When hiking through thick undergrowth with poor visibility, be careful about where you put your feet. Unseen potholes and tree stumps can ruin ankles and trip up weary hikers, resulting in injury and, even worse, pain. Do not be embarrassed to go down extremely steep slopes on your hands and knees.

5. Time

Just remember that you always have less time than you imagine and that everything always takes longer than you expect during a hike. Try and leave as early as possible

DANGERS & ANNOYANCES

1. Emergency helplines

Emergency Helplines are found regularly on Hong Kong's trails and connect you directly to the police in an emergency. Helplines are marked on Countryside Series maps and also on the maps and text of this book. If there is no helpline close by, call 999 to contact the police.

2. Dehydration

I think I've already said enough about water, just wanted to put this in to re-emphasise my point. Just make sure you bring enough.

3. Injuries

If you feel tired, weak, unwell or have injured yourself, do not try to be brave and continue your hike. Consult your map and find the simplest route down from the hiking route and back into civilisation. If necessary, seek professional help and attention immediately. Do not try to be a hero/heroine.

4. Getting lost

If you get lost then please stop immediately and retrace your steps to the last place where you were certain of your location. Do not continue when you are lost hoping to rejoin your path. Always turn back.

5. Stray dogs

These are seen often, sometimes in some of the most remote locations imaginable. These dogs will often follow you, stare at you and bark at you aggressively. The best tactic is to ignore them and continue along your path, they will usually shy away. If they do actually physically attack you (which has never happened to me), don't be intimidated and get to a safe location as soon as possible.

6. Monkeys

Hong Kong plays host to long-tailed and rhesus macaque monkeys. In some areas the monkey population has risen grossly beyond natural proportions. In these areas, monkeys regularly follow people, stealing loose plastic bags or any item that might contain food. Although attacks are rare they are not unheard of. The best technique when walking past monkeys is to ignore them and to maintain a brisk, unfaltering pace.

7. Snakes

Snakes are commonly encountered in Hong Kong, especially during summer. Snakes will only bite if you catch them by surprise or scare them. If you encounter one, just leave it alone. Making lots of noise and creating vibrations whilst walking can help to scare snakes away, and if you have a walking stick you can use it to tap the ground in front of you on overgrown paths. Rugged boots can offer protection in case of a bite. Please consult a **First Aid book** on the best way to treat a snake bite, as the author is not qualified to give this information.

8. Weather

Hong Kong weather can be unpredictable, particularly in the summer. Please be properly prepared for any eventuality. Spare clothes and sun cream are always essentials. You can check the forecast at **http://www.hko.gov.hk/wxinfo/currwx/fnd.htm**

9. Hill fires

Hill fires are common in Hong Kong. If you see a hill fire then please get out of the countryside to safety as soon as possible. Once safe you can call 999 and inform the police of the fire.

10. Robberies

Robberies are very rare. If you are robbed on a hike then you really are very unlucky. If this situation does occur don't try to be brave. Give them what they want, don't argue and once they leave go back to civilisation and call the police on 999.

11. Litter

More of an annoyance than a danger, litter is the scourge of the countryside. Please take all your litter with you when you leave the countryside. Don't contribute to this unsightly problem.

LEGAL DISCLAIMER

Any person continuing beyond this page of the book, regardless of if they have read the legal disclaimer or not, accepts that they, or anyone accompanying them, embark on all the hikes in this book at their own risk and that the author does not assume and hereby disclaims any liability to any party for any loss, injury or damage caused by any activities associated with the use of this book. The author does not assume and hereby disclaims any liability to any party for any loss, injury or damage caused due to the use of this book, regardless of whether that party is aware of the intended target audience for this book or not. Opinions and interpretations expressed in this book are those of the author who has made every effort to ensure the information in this book was correct at the time of going to press, however the author does not assume and hereby disclaims any liability to any party for any loss or damage caused by errors, omissions or misleading information, whether such errors or omissions result from negligence, accident or any other cause.

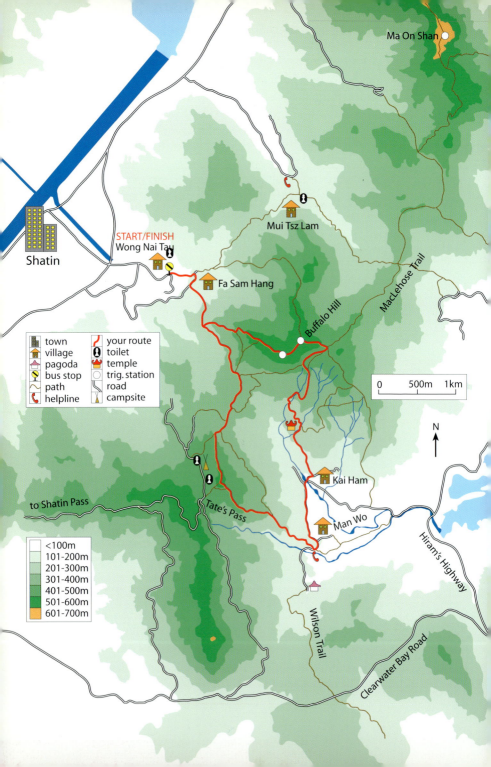

HIKE 1: Wong Nai Tau round trip

summary:

12.17km ・ **5½h** ・ **Sai Kung & Clear Water Bay**

starting point: 黃泥頭

Wong Nai Tau bus terminus

getting to start: Shatin + 65A or $40

Go to Sha Tin KCR station. Take green mini bus 65A (HK$3.7) from Sha Tin central (see Appendix, A-ii for instructions on how to get to bus stop) or a red taxi (about HK$40) to Wong Nai Tau.

description:

The hike starts at Wong Nai Tau and climbs West Buffalo Hill and Buffalo Hill. From here it goes briefly down to the MacLehose trail before following a narrow path down past a temple to Kai Ham. From here the path takes the Wilson trail up to Tung Yeung Shan, before once again briefly joining the MacLehose Trail and then heading all the way back down to Wong Nai Tau.

getting home: 65A or $40 + Shatin

Take green mini bus 65A (HK$3.7) or a red taxi (about HK$40) from Wong Nai Tau to Sha Tin KCR station.

WARNINGS:

Attempting this hike in wet weather is not recommended. The descent from Buffalo Hill is overgrown and steep. Sections of the hike are quite slippery and the path becomes extremely overgrown in places. Expect to be pushing your way through at least one very thick bamboo grove.

hike Xsection:

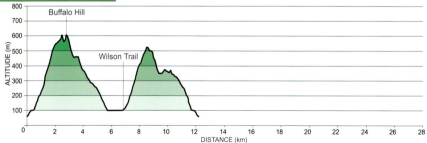

GETTING TO START Take the KCR to Shatin. Take green mini bus 65A (HK$3.7) or a red taxi (about HK$40) to Wong Nai Tau.

START

Stand facing the road you just arrived on, which is 'Siu Lek Yuen Road'. Climb the stairs to your left which begin from next to the small KMB information booth, (Figure 1).

Figure 1: Climb the stairs which begin next to the KMB information booth.

0.04 Continue straight ahead along the concrete path, signposted 'Fa Sam Hang Village'. Ignore the path to your right signposted 'Tai Che Village'. Ignore any smaller paths to your left or right.

0.34 Turn right at the road.

0.47 **ATTENTION** Turn left off the road, taking the narrow concrete path which climbs gradually, (Figure 2). Do not continue straight ahead down the hill along the road.

Figure 2: Turn left off the road along the concrete path.

0.49 Turn left after about 20m, climbing the hill. This is the second path to your left after leaving the road. You passed the first path, which leads to a small farm, about 10m before this turning.

0.61 Continue straight ahead up the hill, along the path which soon becomes stairs. Ignore the path continuing straight ahead towards the right.

0.69 Turn right, signposted 'Shek Nga Pui', leaving the path you are on which soon becomes very overgrown. Your path will soon begin to climb more steeply.

1.10 **ATTENTION** Turn sharp left, climbing the hill along the narrow path which begins soon after your path emerges from the woodland, **(Figure 3)**. You leave the main path at this point. There is a small path to your right about 4 metres before your path climbs to the left, you can use this as a marker.

Continue up the hill, ignoring any smaller paths to the left or right which may go down. Your path will eventually lead to the top of West Buffalo Hill.

Figure 3: Take the narrow path which climbs steeply to your left.

2.43 ****TRIG. STATION** Continue straight ahead down the hill** at the trigonometrical station on top of West Buffalo Hill.

2.61 **Continue straight ahead up the hill** at the next junction, towards the peak of Buffalo Hill. Ignore the small path to your right.

2.77 ****TRIG. STATION** Turn right just after the trigonometrical station,** following the narrow path down the hill. This path may be overgrown but is always possible to follow. Ignore the path to your left.

3.21 **Turn right at the bottom of the hill** along the clear mud path, signposted 'Gilwell Campsite'. You are now on the MacLehose trail. Ignore the paths to your left and straight ahead of you.

3.43 **You pass mileage post M089 about 220m after turning right.**

3.61 ****ATTENTION** Turn left about 180m after mileage post M089, following the narrow mud path steeply down the hill,** **(Figure 4)**. This mud path may be difficult to find. It begins about 20m after passing a small cave on your right. The main path bends towards the right about 10m after your path goes down to the left.

Continue along the narrow path you are on, which might be very overgrown in places.

Figure 4: Take the steep, muddy path down the hill to your left.

After about 490m you pass a small cluster of rocks and then immediately enter a woodland. 30m after this the clearest path bends around to the left (ignore the minor path straight ahead of you). Beyond this point the path becomes extremely overgrown in places and you pass through a thick, dense bamboo grove. It may be easier for you to crouch low to the ground at this point, below the dense foliage there is a clear tunnel. The path always remains possible to follow.

4.59   **Turn right at the large stream,** do not cross the stream. The rocky path you are on heads down the hill. Do not walk towards the small temples.

Continue along the rocky path which crosses the stream, passes through a small, derelict village and then runs next to the stream for a while.

5.42   **Follow the steps down to the right,** ignoring the concrete slope with the rope directly ahead of you.

5.65   **Turn right at the road.** You emerge near Kai Ham village.

5.80   **Turn right, crossing the large bridge with the blue railings,** signposted 'Man Wo Village' amongst other things. Do not continue straight ahead.

6.55   Continue along the road you are on, ignoring the turning to your left signposted 'Man Wo Village' amongst other things.

6.82   ****ATTENTION** Turn right off the road, crossing the narrow bridge with the blue railings.** Follow the path to the right after crossing the bridge. You are near an **emergency helpline.** Your path is signposted 'Wilson Trail' and soon starts to climb.

Follow the path around to the right after 60m, passing the small house on your left. 20m later the path continues up the hill to your left, as the concrete path directly ahead of you peters out.

6.98   You pass mileage post W037 on your right. Continue along the Wilson Trail, ignoring any smaller paths to your left or right.

8.37   **Continue straight ahead up the hill, (Figure 5),** at the clear junction with the crumbling concrete block labelled 'Wilson Trail'. Ignore the paths going around the hill to your left and down the hill to your right.

8.53 Turn right at the top of the hill, ignoring the path to your left. This path will generally continue down the hill. It may be overgrown but is always possible to follow.

9.18 Turn right along the wide mud path at the bottom of the hill. You are now on the MacLehose trail and emerge almost directly next to mileage post M093.

Figure 5: Continue straight ahead up the hill at the junction.

9.69 You pass mileage post M092 on your right.

10.13 **ATTENTION** 440m after mileage post M092 your path reaches a rocky area similar to a river bed. Turn left off the MacLehose trail, signposted 'Fa Sam Hang', following the clear mud path up the hill sharply to

Figure 6: Turn left off the MacLehose trail.

the left, (Figure 6). Ignore your current path which bends slightly towards the right. If you reach mileage post M091 on your left you have gone about 60m too far along the MacLehose trail.

Continue along this path which climbs a small hill and then goes downhill. Ignore any smaller paths which may branch off it. After 960m you pass the path you took earlier towards Buffalo Hill.

11.48 Turn left, following the stairs down the hill. Follow this path to the right after about 200m, down to the road.

11.70 Turn right at the road.

11.83 Turn left next to the lamp post and red fire hydrant, following the narrow concrete path you took earlier, which runs between the two fences and leads to Wong Nai Tau bus depot again.

12.17 **FINISH**

GETTING HOME Take green mini bus 65A (HK$3.7) or a red taxi (about HK$40) to Shatin KCR station.

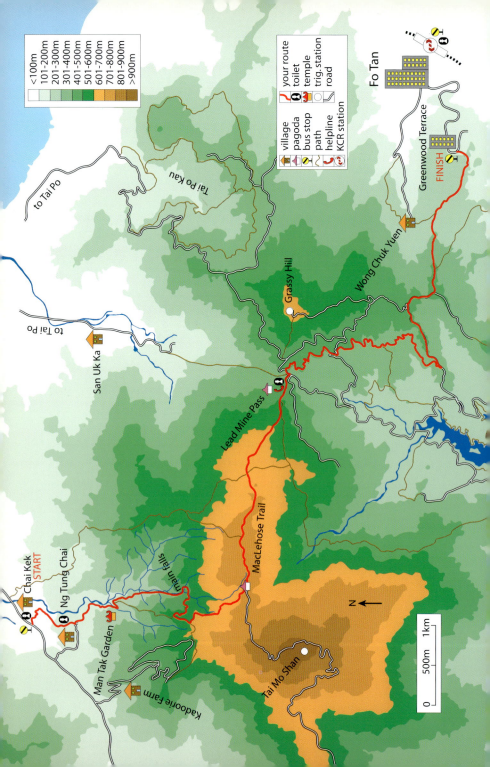

Legend:

<100m	
101-200m	
201-300m	
301-400m	
401-500m	
501-600m	
601-700m	
701-800m	
801-900m	
>900m	

your route
toilet
temple
trig. station
road

village
pagoda
bus stop
path
helpline
KCR station

Fo Tan

Greenwood Terrace

FINISH

Wong Chuk Yuen

Grassy Hill

to Tai Po

Tai Po Kau

to Tai Po

San Uk Ka

Lead Mine Pass

MacLehose Trail

main falls

Chai Kek

START

Ng Tung Chai

Man Tak Garden

Kadoorie Farm

Tai Mo Shan

N

0   500m   1km

Hike 2: Chai Kek Village to Sui Wo Road

summary:

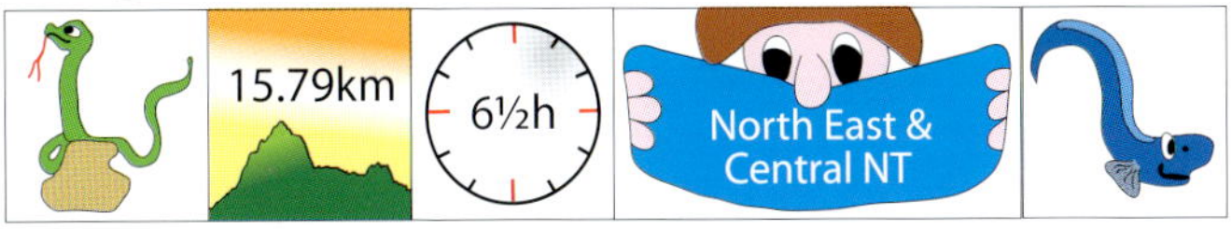
15.79km
6½h
North East &
Central NT

starting point: 寨乪 巴士站

Chai Kek Village bus stop

getting to start: Tai Po Market + 64K or $55

Go to Tai Po Market KCR station. Take bus 64K (HK$6.9) or a taxi (about HK$55) to Chai Kek Village bus stop, which is on the main road. Please ask where to get off as Chai Kek is not the terminus for the 64K bus. (More info. Appendix A-iii).

description:

The hike starts at Chai Kek Village and winds its way up the hills, passing Ng Tung Chai waterfalls. Continuing to the base of Tai Mo Shan, we walk down to Lead Mine Pass before following a secretive contour path. After this we walk uphill for a while before joining the MacLehose Trail. Soon after we turn left, and the hike goes downhill towards Fo Tan, ending at Sui Wo Road.

getting home: 69K or $40 + Shatin or $25 + Fo Tan

From Sui Wo Road, green mini bus 69K (HK$5.2) goes to Sha Tin KCR towards your left. Fo Tan is the closest KCR by taxi (about HK$25), but Shatin is only slightly further away, (about HK$40).

WARNINGS:

Attempting this hike in wet weather is not recommended. Sections of the hike are rocky and mossy and may become extremely slippery and dangerous. One of the paths has a 'Road Closed' sign before it. Please note, you continue past this sign AT YOUR OWN RISK.

hike Xsection:

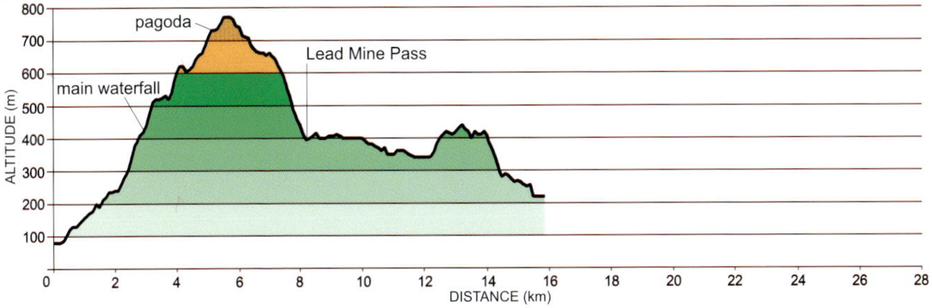
pagoda
Lead Mine Pass
main waterfall
ALTITUDE (m)
800
700
600
500
400
300
200
100
0
2
4
6
8
10
12
14
16
18
20
22
24
26
28
DISTANCE (km)

GETTING TO START Take the KCR to Tai Po Market. Take bus number 64K (HK$6.9), or a taxi (about HK$55) to Chai Kek Village.

START

Climb the steps going up to your left next to the 64K bus stop, signposted 'Chai Kek Village'.

Turn right along the concrete path.

Turn left at the wide village access road.

0.07 Turn right, following the main path. You will pass house number 31D on your left.

Turn left after crossing the small bridge and pass the public toilets on your right.

Follow the path slightly upwards towards your right, ignoring the path towards your left.

0.19 Pass through the small square. You will pass house number 73 on your right.

Turn left after passing through the square, passing the large, newly built village houses on your right.

0.25 **ATTENTION** About 60m after the square, just after passing house number 93 on your right, take the small concrete path found to your right, running directly alongside the house, (Figure 1). This path is well hidden. Do not continue slightly downwards along the wide, concrete road on which you currently find yourself.

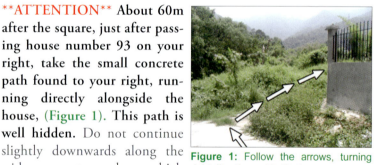

Figure 1: Follow the arrows, turning right directly next to the house.

Continue along the concrete path. You will pass a small altar after about 120m. Ignore the small path going down to your left.

0.42 Turn left at the fork in the path, continuing up the hill. You will pass a small cluster of houses, eventually passing house numbers 37B and 39B on your left.

0.51 **Continue slightly to your right** along the path you are on, ignoring the path to your left. You will pass a toilet on your left and bend round into a small square.

0.69 ****ATTENTION** At the small square, take the concrete path directly in front of you, passing through the gap between house numbers 1 and 2, (Figure 2).** This path may initially be overlooked, but just pass straight thought the square and look for the gap between the houses.

Figure 2: Pass directly between house numbers 1 and 2.

Turn left after 40m, following the path you are already on. Do not follow the path to your right and do not climb the stairs which are straight ahead of you. You will pass house number 41 on your right.

Continue along this path, passing through a small bamboo grove. You soon have your first glimpse of the stream.

1.17 **Pass through the large, conspicuous gate.**

Continue along the narrow path you are on, walking slightly uphill. Ignore the wider path which branches off to the left.

1.44 **Pass the monastery on your right,** continuing over the small bridge and up the hill to the right. There is a sign pointing towards the waterfall.

1.56 **Continue straight ahead** along the mud path with three signposts, 'To Main Fall', 'To Middle Fall', and 'To Bottom Fall'. You pass a map on your right. Ignore the path going sharply up to your right signposted 'Tai Mo Shan'. Ignore any minor paths to your left or right. The path now climbs quite precariously.

2.28 **Continue along the path up the stairs,** signposted 'To Waterfall'. Ignore the path signposted 'Bottom Falls' going down to your left, unless you want to take a quick detour (see photo p.25).

2.40 **Continue towards the right, following the main path steeply upwards.** Ignore the path signposted 'Middle Falls' which continues straight ahead, unless you want to take a quick detour.

2.72 **Continue towards the right,** climbing steeply. Ignore the path directly ahead of you leading to the small waterfall. The path you are on leads to the main falls.

2.93 **At the large, main falls, follow the path around to the left,** crossing the stream and climbing the steps. The crossing can be quite dangerous so be careful, especially in wet or damp weather.

WARNING The Country Parks Authority has placed a 'Road Closed' sign on your path in the belief that it might be dangerous for people to continue. Any inexperienced hikers, or those not happy climbing difficult and potentially slippery terrain should turn back now. YOU CONTINUE AT YOUR OWN RISK.

2.94 **Pass the 'Road Closed' sign, (Figure 3),** and continue up the hill.

Figure 3: Continue along the path, passing the 'Road Closed' sign.

Pass the sign labelled 'Warning Landslide Ahead Please Retrace Your Steps', remembering once again that you continue at your own risk. You will cross a small stream, climb to your right, then a few metres later climb towards the left.

3.02 **Pass the large rock on your left, with your path hidden slightly to the right.**

3.04 **Take a sharp right up the hill,** along the rocky path. Ignore the mud path to your left leading to the small waterfall.

3.07 **Pass the 'Landslide Warning' sign,** which has its back to you. This completes the landslide section of the walk. The path continues past another 'Road Closed' sign.

3.13 **Pass the 'Scatter Falls' on your left,** and the path will begin to climb.

3.19 Continue upwards along the main path to the right.

3.27 **Continue up the main path.** Ignore the small path which veers off to the left. Shortly, you will pass through the old entrance of a small village house, followed by a bamboo grove.

3.70 **Turn sharp left, signposted 'Tai Mo Shan'** at the clearing. There is also a map showing Tai Mo Shan and Shing Mun Country Park. Ignore the path straight ahead of you labelled 'Lam Tam Road'. Your path climbs the hill and crosses a couple of small streams. Ignore any smaller offshoots from the main path.

5.12 **Turn left at the pagoda,** along the mud path to 'Lead Mine Pass'. Ignore the concrete road to your right. You are now on stage 8 of the MacLehose trail and you simply need to follow the trail all the way down to Lead Mine Pass. You will soon pass mileage post M143.

8.22 **Turn left at the road,** after passing through the arch labelled 'MacLehose stage 7'. The road is also signposted as 'MacLehose stage 7'. You pass some toilets on your left hand side.

8.31 ****ATTENTION** On your right is a helicopter landing pad. As you face the pad there is a concrete path starting from the rear left of the landing pad. Take this path, (Figure 4).** The path soon becomes a stone path and will eventually become a mud track.

Figure 4: The arrow indicates the path at the rear of the helicopter pad.

8.36 **Turn right.** Do not pass through the gate labelled 'No Admittance'. Follow the winding, shaded mud path, ignoring any minor animal tracks to your left and right. This path crosses several small streams which may become slippery and flooded when it is raining.

9.41 ****ATTENTION** Turn left at the concrete road. After about 30m take the mud path to your right off the road, going slightly downhill.** The path may be slightly wild and overgrown. Once again, ignore any small animal tracks to your left or right. Do not continue along the concrete road.

10.58 Continue left up the small steep slope. The path will then turn into a sharp muddy downslope. Continue along the winding, twisting path.

12.25 Turn left at the concrete road, walking up the hill. Continue along this road. Don't be disheartened by all the hills.

13.22 Continue straight ahead, slightly to the right at the crossroads, labelled 'Needle Hill'. Ignore the path to your left labelled 'Grassy Hill'. You are now on stage 7 of the MacLehose trail.

13.67 Turn left at the small clearing with benches, passing under the large wooden sign labelled 'To Shatin Town'.

Continue straight ahead, passing the map on your left. This path soon becomes a dirt track.

13.99 Continue straight ahead, signposted 'to Greenwood Terrace'. Ignore the path going down to your right. Your path leads down some steps and under an electricity pylon.

14.74 Continue straight ahead, ignoring the stone and concrete path that goes sharply left, signposted 'Wong Chuk Yeung'.

Continue along the main mud path, ignoring smaller paths to the left or right. You will pass two more pylons and climb a short, steep mud hill.

15.22 Continue along your path, passing the small shelter on your left.

15.33 Turn right at the round water authorities building, following the outside of the building's fence.

Turn right down the steep concrete stairs and at the bottom cross the small bridge.

15.48 Climb the small stairs slightly to your right and follow the concrete path straight ahead of you, ignoring the two sets of steps which go down to your right. Follow this path until you reach a small concrete clearing in front of a large housing estate.

Turn left along the access road at this clearing. This road will soon reach the larger Sui Wo Road, signalling the end of the hike.

15.79 **FINISH**

GETTING HOME Take green mini bus 69K (HK$5.2) in the direction of your left as you arrive at the road. This bus goes to Shatin KCR station. You can also take a taxi, either to Fo Tan KCR (about HK$25) or Shatin KCR station (about HK$40).

The bottom falls at Ng Tung Chai offer a prelude of what is to come!!

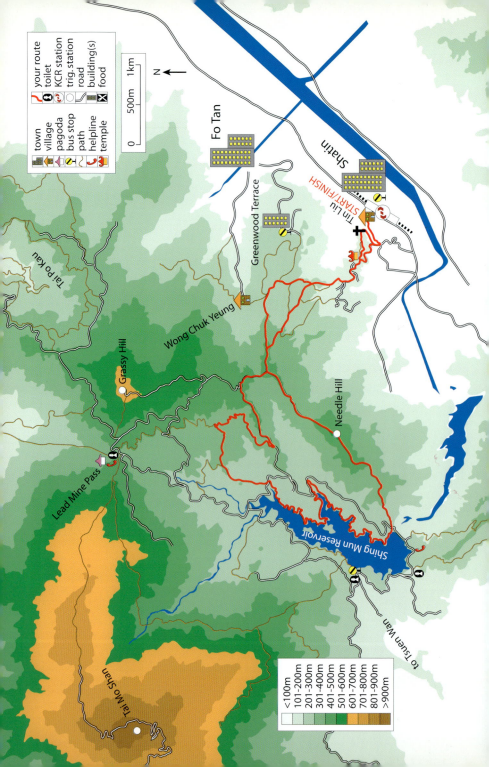

Legend

your route	toilet	KCR station	trig. station	road
building(s)	food			

town	village	pagoda	bus stop	path	helpline	temple

N

0   500m   1km

Fo Tan

Shatin

Tin Liu

START/FINISH

Greenwood Terrace

Tai Po Kau

Wong Chuk Yeung

Grassy Hill

Needle Hill

Lead Mine Pass

Shing Mun Reservoir

Tai Mo Shan

to Tsuen Wan

<100m	
101–200m	
201–300m	
301–400m	
401–500m	
501–600m	
601–700m	
701–800m	
801–900m	
>900m	

HIKE 3: Shatin round trip

summary:

20.55km 7h North East & Central NT

starting point: 沙田火車站

Shatin KCR station

getting to start: Shatin

Go to Shatin KCR station.

description:

The hike starts at Shatin KCR and passes through a village before climbing to a large cross with a dramatic view. We then pass a temple complex before beginning a long climb which ends at the MacLehose trail. We now walk over Needle Hill before following the Shing Mun jogging trail for 5km. After this we follow a hidden path which contains an overgrown climb before rejoining the MacLehose trail briefly and then walking back down to Shatin KCR.

getting home: Shatin

Take the KCR from Shatin station.

WARNINGS:

Be careful of steep eroded paths near the beginning of the hike. These may be dangerous to navigate. Ignore any monkeys you might see at Shing Mun Reservoir and do not try to interact with them. Look out for eroded ravines on the mud paths towards the end of the hike.

hike Xsection:

km from start	

GETTING TO START Take the KCR to Shatin station.

START

Take the exit leading to the bus depot and turn left, you will then pass the bus depot on your right. If you take the exit leading into the shopping plaza, turn left and then left again at the bus depot and you will pass the aforementioned exit on your left.

0.05 **Turn right and walk down the large concrete pedestrian walkway.** This is signposted 'Heritage Museum' amongst other things.

0.14 **Turn sharp left as soon as you reach the bottom of the ramp.** You must turn left inbetween the end of the ramp and the map. You will be on a concrete path with yellow railings and will pass a village square on your right.

0.19 **Continue straight ahead for about 50m then climb the concrete stairs going up the hill slightly to your right, (Figure 1).** Ignore the steps leading to the private houses and the concrete path to your left.

Figure 1: Take the steps leading up the hill through the village.

Continue along this main path. Ignore any smaller paths or steps that may branch off to your left or right.

0.75 **Turn right at the large road with the roundabout.** This road is 'To Fung Shan Road'.

0.87 **After about 120m turn right up the concrete stairs,** signposted 'Ascension House'.

0.93 **Take the path going to the right at the fork in the path,** once again signposted 'Ascension House'. You will pass Ascension House on your right as the path climbs upwards. Ignore the small path leading off to your left.

1.17 **You will reach a clearing with a large, white cross.**

1.21 **Pass through the white gate with Chinese characters written on it about 40m to your left.** Continue upwards along the concrete path.

1.25 **Turn left along the mud path** at the top of the hill, this will soon become a paved path. Ignore any steps or paths going down to your left.

1.42 **Climb the steps to your right** leading to a complex with a large temple directly in front of you.

ATTENTION Please respect the tranquility of this area, especially if your group is quite large.

1.45 **Turn left at the large pagoda, passing through a small round archway, (Figure 2).** Continue through the small garden with a fountain and through the second small round archway.

1.47 **Turn left,** along the path towards the lotus pond.

Continue straight ahead, down the steps past the lotus pond and through the small clearing.

Figure 2: Pass through this small, round archway.

1.57 **Turn right at the road.** Continue straight ahead along the road. Ignore any smaller roads or driveways going off to the left or right. This road will twist and turn up the hill. You will pass through a small village. The road then starts climbing and you will see the white buildings of the 'Lutheran Theological Seminary' on your right.

2.00 ****ATTENTION**** Directly in front of you is a large gate, wide enough for cars to drive through, signposted 'Consulate of the Kingdom of Morrocco'. Follow the small path straight ahead just to the left of this gate which runs alongside the fence, **(Figure 3).** Do not follow the main road as it bends down

Figure 3: Follow the path just to the left of the main gate.

the hill to your left.

Continue along the mud path which climbs upwards, do not take the concrete driveway which turns off to your left. Ignore any stairs or smaller paths which branch off from the path you are on.

2.29 **Continue straight ahead, signposted 'to MacLehose Trail', climbing steeply up the hill.** Do not take the larger path leading to your left. There are a few makeshift shelters at this junction.

Pass throught the clearing, continuing downwards along the path.

2.55 **Continue straight ahead on the central path, steeply uphill, at the junction with the old signpost where there are three paths you could take.** Do not take the paths to your left or right which both lead slightly downhill. The path you are on is very eroded.

3.03 **At the pylon take the path leading to your left,** which will eventually continue up the hill. This path is also very eroded.

3.67 **Turn left at the top of the hill, signposted 'to MacLehose Trail'.** You are still on a mud path. Ignore the path to your right.

3.99 **Turn left at the road,** in the direction of Needle Hill. You are now on the MacLehose trail. You will have passed through a large sign saying 'Welcome to Shing Mun Country Park'.

4.78 Conintue straight ahead at the end of the road, walking along the small path and climbing Needle Hill.

5.26 ****TRIG. STATION** Continue straight ahead in the same direction, beginning the descent of Needle Hill.** This trail will twist and turn a bit but generally heads down towards Shing Mun Reservoir.

7.04 **Turn left at the road,** after passing through the 'MacLehose Stage 7' sign. The road soon bends sharply towards the right. The small stairs in front of you end up at the same place. You are now at Shing Mun Reservoir main dam.

7.18 ****ATTENTION** Continue straight ahead along the small concrete path, signposted 'Wilson Trail' and also 'Jogging Trail', passing along the right side of the reservoir. DO NOT turn left**

across the main dam. Your path soon becomes a dirt track.

Continue along this path for the next 5km, until the end of the jogging trail.

12.20 ****ATTENTION** At the road, turn right, walk about 10m and then turn left. Immediately on your left follow the 9 concrete stairs twisting up the side of the hill, (Figure 4).** This path soon becomes quite a broad mud path.

12.91 ****ATTENTION**** **At the minor junction between three paths, continue straight ahead along the small, overgrown path which climbs steeply up the hill, (Figure 5).** Do not take the main path which goes down to your left or the small overgrown path leading down to your right.

Figure 4: Follow the concrete stairs up the side of the hill.

13.20 **Continue straight ahead** along your path, ignoring the unclear path to your right. Your path will itself eventually bend around to the right. The path is overgrown but can be followed. Be careful not to lose the main path by accidentally taking small animal tracks to your left or right.

Figure 5: Take the central path, which leads up the hill.

13.60 **Turn right at the clear intersection with a wide mud path** and follow the path down the steep muddy hill. Do not turn to the left, also down a steep, muddy hill.

15.12 **Turn left at the concrete road,** walking up the hill. Continue along this road. Don't be disheartened by all the hills.

16.13 **Continue straight ahead, slightly to the right at the crossroads in the direction labelled 'Needle Hill'.** Ignore the path to your left labelled 'Grassy Hill'. You are now on stage 7 of the MacLehose trail again.

16.54 **Turn left at the small clearing with benches.** Pass through the large wooden arch labelled 'To Shatin Town' and continue along the small path which runs past the map. This path is quite narrow and begins as a mixture of concrete and rocks but soon becomes a mud path.

16.90 **Continue straight ahead, signposted 'to Greenwood Terrace'** at the junction with the old signpost. Ignore the path going down the hill to your right which you arrived on earlier. Your path leads down some steps and under an electricity pylon.

17.62 ****ATTENTION** Continue straight ahead, in the direction 'Sui Wo Road', at the junction with the concrete and rock path going sharply to your left to 'Wong Chuk Yeung Village'. Please TAKE NOTE of this junction.**

17.80 ****ATTENTION** Turn right along the narrow mud path about 180m after the above mentioned junction,** (Figure 6). It is found at the bottom of a small hill, and goes downwards. Do not climb the steep muddy slope ahead of you slightly towards the left.

Figure 6: Follow this narrow mud path down towards the right.

18.02 **Continue along your path,** down the hill. Ignore the path going back up the hill to your left.

18.04 ****WARNING** Please be careful of the narrow but deep eroded ravine running directly across the middle of the path.**

Cross the two small bridges.

18.08 **Turn left,** around the side of the hill at the junction with the old signpost, ignoring the path to your right.

18.35 **Turn left again,** at the next junction with yet another old signpost. You once again pass through the clearing you encountered at the start of the hike.

18.61 **Turn left,** at the bottom of the stairs along the mud path, ignoring the path to your right.

Continue straight ahead, ignoring the steps that lead up to your right and the decrepit concrete road also leading to your right. Once again follow the small path running alongside the fence and down to the road.

18.90 **Turn left at the road.** Continue along the main road ignoring any minor offshoots or side roads. The road twists and turns down the hill.

19.89 **Turn left at the roundabout,** following the small concrete path with green railings, which you walked up earlier today. The path goes down through the village. It is signposted 'Shatin KCR Station' at the information point.

20.36 **Continue straight ahead slightly to your left,** passing the village square on your left hand side.

20.41 **Turn sharp right and start walking up the concrete pedestrian walkway.**

20.50 **Turn left** at the top of the walkway. Shatin KCR station will be on your right after about 50m.

20.55 ****FINISH****

GETTING HOME Take the KCR from Shatin station.

The serene, pagoda-like church seen near the beginning of this hike.

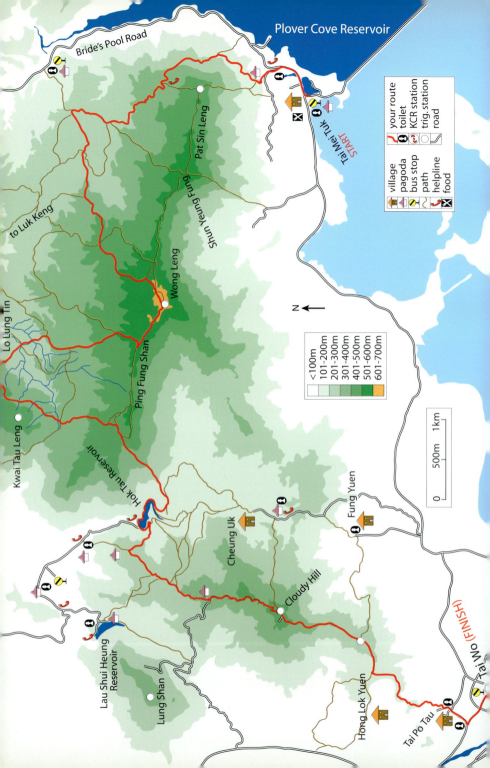

Plover Cove Reservoir

Bride's Pool Road

to Luk Keng

Lo Lung Tin

START

Tai Mei Tuk

Pat Sin Leng

Shun Yeung Fung

Wong Leng

Ping Fung Shan

Hok Tau Reservoir

Kwai Tau Leng

Cheung Uk

Fung Yuen

Cloudy Hill

Lau Shui Heung Reservoir

Lung Shan

Hong Lok Yuen

Tai Po Tau

Tai Wo (FINISH)

N

<100m
101-200m
201-300m
301-400m
401-500m
501-600m
601-700m

0   500m   1km

village
pagoda
bus stop
path
helpline
food

your route
toilet
KCR station
trig. station
road

HIKE 4: Tai Mei Tuk to Tai Wo KCR via Lo Lung Tin

summary:

| | 23.11km | 7½h | North East & Central NT | | |

starting point: 大尾篤總站

Tai Mei Tuk bus terminus

getting to start: Tai Po Market + 20C or 75K or $60

Take the KCR to Tai Po Market KCR station. Take green mini bus 20C (HK$6), bus 75K (HK$4.7) or a green taxi (about HK$60) to Tai Mei Tuk. (More info. Appendix A-iii).

description:

The hike starts at Tai Mei Tuk and follows the Pat Sin Leng family walk for a short while before briefly climbing up close to Wong Leng. On Ping Fung Shan we follow a narrow, very slippery path down to Lo Lung Tin before heading to Ping Teng Au and then climbing steadily up to the ridge close to Ping Fung Shan. From here the route goes down to Hok Tau Reservoir, following the Wilson Trail over Cloudy Hill and down to Tai Wo KCR station.

getting home: Tai Wo

Take the KCR from Tai Wo station.

WARNINGS:

This hike is not recommended in wet weather. The path leading from Ping Fung Shan down to Lo Lung Tin is extremely slippery, containing many moss covered areas. This path is also overgrown and steep in places.

hike Xsection:

km from start	

GETTING TO START Take the KCR to Tai Po Market station. Take green mini bus 20C (HK$6), bus number 75K (HK$4.7) or a taxi (about HK$60) to Tai Mei Tuk.

START

From the bus stop or taxi rank, face the main, tarmaced road along which you just arrived.

Walk to this main, tarmaced road and turn right, following the road. Ignore any turnings to your left or right. You are walking in the direction of the Pat Sin Leng nature trail.

0.67 At the top of the hill leave the tarmaced road and follow the smaller, concrete road up the hill slightly towards your left, signposted 'Pat Sin Leng Nature Trail', **(Figure 1).** You will have passed the visitor centre driveway on your left just before leaving the road and the 'Agriculture, Fisheries and Conservation Department, Plover Cove Country Park, Tai Mei Tuk Management Centre' sign on your right. The path bends to the left up the hill. Do not follow 'Bride's Pool Road' down the hill.

Figure 1: Leave the main road, heading up towards the nature trail.

0.76 Turn right, crossing the concrete bridge with the blue railings. You will pass under a sign labelled 'Pat Sin Leng Nature Trail'. Do not continue along the road up the hill.

Continue up the steps along the nature trail. You will pass through the 'Spring Breeze Pavilion Memorial' after about 100m and also pass regular numbered nature trail posts.

1.05 Ignore the steep path to your left marked with 'Danger' and 'Warning' signs.

1.72 Continue along the nature trail, signposted 'Wan Shan Keuk'. Ignore the path to your right labelled 'Bride's Pool Road'.

2.71 Continue along the main path, which bends to the left, at the junction with the **emergency helpline.** This is signposted 'Bride's Pool' and you are now on the Wilson trail. Do not go sharply left up the hill to Pat Sin Leng. Ignore the small mud path to your right.

2.86 Cross the stream, following the path around to the right. You will soon pass nature trail post number 15 and Wilson trail mileage post W127.

3.53 Continue along the nature trail after crossing the narrow stream near post W128.

3.75 Cross the wide stream, following the path around to the right.

4.06 **Continue straight ahead, slightly to the right at the junction, signposted 'Bride's Pool'.** Do not turn left along the Wilson trail, signposted 'Luk Keng'.

4.45 **Cross the stream and continue up the steps towards the left** along the nature trail. Do not follow any mud paths just before crossing the stream or the path to your right just after crossing the stream.

4.60 **Turn left, signposted 'Luk Keng',** along the clear mud path. Do not continue straight ahead along the main path, signposted 'Bride's Pool'. You will cross a stream after about 540m.

5.26 **Continue straight ahead at the junction,** along the clear mud path signposted 'Pat Sin Leng'. Ignore the paths to your right and left, signposted 'Luk Keng' and 'Bride's Pool' respectively.

6.66 **Continue towards the left at the junction, signposted 'Pat Sin Leng'.** Ignore the path going down the hill to your right, signposted 'Luk Keng'.

7.60 **Turn right at the junction, signposted 'Hok Tau'.** Ignore the path to your left signposted 'Pat Sin Leng'.

7.82 **Continue straight ahead slightly to the right along the path signposted 'Hok Tau'.** Ignore the path leading sharply to your left, signposted 'Pat Sin Leng'.

7.98 **Continue straight ahead, signposted 'Hok Tau'.** Ignore the paths leading to your left and right. You are now on the Wilson Trail.

8.40 Continue towards the right along the main path, do not climb over the small hill directly ahead of you.

WARNING The next path is extremely slippery and is responsible for the eel rating. Please take extreme care on this path.

8.55 ****ATTENTION**** STOP when you reach a sign on your left labelled 'Hok Tau Reservoir' and 'Pat Sin Leng'. Turn RIGHT down the small, unclear, overgrown path directly opposite this sign, (Figure 2). You will be leaving the main path at this point.

Figure 2: Turn right off the main path at the signpost.

8.70 ****ATTENTION**** Turn left at the tiny junction found about 150m after turning onto the small path. DO NOT continue straight ahead. This junction is very easy to miss. Your path remains overgrown and slippery but is always possible to follow.

8.97 Turn left about 270m after the last tiny junction, following the small path down the hill. Ignore the other path, which continues straight ahead. Your path becomes extremely overgrown after about 280m but always remains possible to follow.

9.70 Continue straight ahead at the junction, along the clear mud path. Ignore the path sharply to your left going down the hill.

10.10 ****ATTENTION**** Turn left down the hill along the small overgrown path. Ignore the clearer path which leads towards your right. Continue along the path you are on, ignoring the even smaller path to your left after about 200m.

10.34 Your path begins to run alongside a small stream, through a bamboo grove. Continue along your main path, ignoring any smaller paths to your left or right.

10.48 ****ATTENTION**** Turn sharp right at the wide stream, following the clear rocky path down the hill alongside the main river bed, which lies to your left, (Figure 3).

Figure 3: Follow the rocky path down the hill alongside the river bed.

10.50 Turn left at the clear main path. After 10m you will cross a concrete bridge which bends around to the right. Soon afterwards you will pass a signpost labelled 'Hok Tau'. You are now on the 'Nam Chung Country Trail'. Ignore any smaller paths to your left or right.

12.33 Continue straight ahead, signposted 'Pat Sin Range'. Ignore the small path to your left.

12.36 Turn sharp left up the wide mud path signposted 'Pat Sin Leng'. Do not continue straight ahead towards 'Tan Chuk Hang'.

13.01 ****ATTENTION**** Turn right along the narrow mud path heading up the hill, (Figure 4). Do not continue along the main path which bends towards the left and ignore the much smaller path leading sharply to your right.

13.23 Turn right at the clear main path. You are now on the Wilson trail once again and will follow it all the way to Tai Wo.

Figure 4: Turn right up the hill, leaving the main path.

13.77 Continue straight ahead down the hill, signposted 'Hok Tau'.

14.41 Turn right, signposted 'Hok Tau', at the large junction at the bottom of the hill. Do not turn left, signposted 'Ping Shan Chai'.

Continue along the main path down the hill. Ignore any paths branching off it. Your path will bend around to the right after about 320m and then passes under a sign labelled 'Hok Tau Family Walk' 30m later. Soon after this the path bends around to the left and you reach the wide road next to the reservoir.

14.82 Turn right at the road, near mileage post W113. You cross a dam after about 460m.

15.45 Continue straight ahead up the steep steps with the blue railings, signposted 'Sha Lo Tung' and 'Hok Tau Family Walk'. Ignore the road as it bends around to the right.

15.69 Turn right up the hill signposted, 'Lau Shui Heung Reservoir'.

Do not continue along the family walk, signposted 'Sha Lo Tung'. Ignore any minor paths leaving the main path.

16.72 **Turn left along the clear mud path, signposted 'Cloudy Hill'.** Ignore the steps straight ahead of you and the path to your right, signposted 'Lau Shui Heung Reservoir'.

16.96 Continue slightly to the right at mileage post W109, ignoring the smaller path straight ahead.

17.65 **Turn left up the concrete road,** signposted 'Cloudy Hill', just after passing the pagoda to your right. Ignore the smaller road sharply to your left and the road to your right.

18.89 Continue along the concrete road, ignoring the path to your left signposted 'Sha Lo Tung'.

19.02 **Turn left along the narrow, concrete path.** Do not continue along the road. You pass a silver map labelled 'Wilson Trail' after about 20m and your path then continues down the hill.

20.20 ****TRIG. STATION**** **Continue straight ahead along the main path.** Ignore any smaller paths to your left or right.

20.69 **Turn left, signposted 'Tai Po Tau Village',** staying on the main path. Do not go right towards the benches.

20.93 **Follow the main path towards the left** just after mileage post W101, continuing down the hill. The path becomes green with a reddish brown border. Continue in the direction of 'Tai Po Tau Village' at the signpost. You will pass a couple of pagodas.

22.04 **Turn left along the concrete path** after the main green path leads down into a **village.** Your path runs alongside a broken up concrete road.

22.09 **Turn right at the clear, large road,** there is a signpost labelled 'Tai Po Tau'. You will pass a toilet and mileage post W99 to your left.

22.15 **Continue straight ahead along the road you are on, signposted 'Tai Po Tau Drive'.** Ignore 'Tai Po Tau Road' to your left. You can walk along the path next to the village houses on your right if you want more tranquility.

22.38 **Turn right along the small side road, signposted 'Subway'.** Ignore the road you were on as it bends around to the left.

22.41	Turn left, going through the subway, signposted 'Wilson Trail'.
22.44	**Turn left** along the pavement next to the main road.
22.71	**Continue straight ahead at the large intersection, crossing the large road ahead of you. Make sure you stay on the same side of the road.** There are no pedestrian lights straight ahead so you will need to cross the road to your right, then cross to your left and then cross to your left again in order to end up on the other side of the road ahead of you.
22.80	**Continue straight ahead, walking alongside 'Po Nga Road'.**
23.02	**Go up the escalator directly ahead of you,** just as you reach the bus depot on your right.
23.07	**Turn right at the top of the escalator.**
	Tai Wo KCR station is now on your left hand side.
23.11	****FINISH****
	GETTING HOME Take the KCR from Tai Wo KCR station.

The view along the ridge from close to Pat Sin Leng is impressive, yet as the sign proves, there are some steep drops close by.

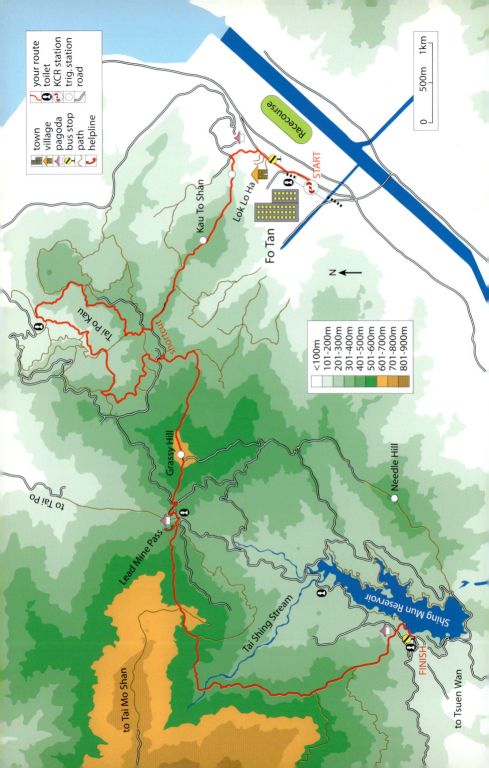

Legend:

your route
toilet
KCR station
trig. station
road

town
village
pagoda
bus stop
path
helpline

Racecourse

START

Fo Tan

Lok Lo Ha

Kau To Shan

Tai Po Kau

shortcut

N

	<100m
	101-200m
	201-300m
	301-400m
	401-500m
	501-600m
	601-700m
	701-800m
	801-900m

Grassy Hill

to Tai Po

Lead Mine Pass

to Tai Mo Shan

Tai Shing Stream

Needle Hill

Shing Mun Reservoir

FINISH

to Tsuen Wan

0   500m   1km

HIKE 5: Fo Tan to Shing Mun Reservoir

summary:

20.16km 7½h North East & Central NT

starting point: 火炭火車站

Fo Tan KCR station

getting to start: Fo Tan

Go to Fo Tan KCR station.

description:

The hike starts at Fo Tan KCR and passes Lok Lo Ha village before climbing up Kau To Shan. There then follows a short detour into Tai Po Kau nature reserve, which can be left out if desired, before Grassy Hill is climbed. From Grassy Hill the route goes down to Lead Mine Pass and from there draws a large circle around to Shing Mun Reservoir, crossing Tai Shing stream on the way whilst following some atmospheric trails.

getting home: 82 or $30 + Tsuen Wan

Take green mini bus 82 or a red taxi (about HK$30) from Shing Mun reservoir to Tsuen Wan. To get to the MTR, walk 4m to the corner, turn left along 'Chung On Street', then turn left again. Climb the flyover 50m ahead of you, cross the main road and continue straight ahead to the MTR station.

WARNINGS:

This hike is not recommended in wet weather. Some paths on this hike are difficult to find and overgrown with ferns which can leave nasty scratches on legs and arms, so long trousers and sleeves might be a good idea. The path up Grassy Hill is rugged and steep. The path leading off the MacLehose trail from Lead Mine Pass is covered in slippery and treacherous rocks. Crossing Tai Shing stream can also be potentially dangerous, especially in the wet. If you encounter monkeys, please ignore them and walk past at a brisk pace.

hike Xsection:

GETTING TO START Take the KCR to Fo Tan station.

START (all distances are measured starting from exit C).

Take either exit A or exit C and turn left. If you take exit A, after you turn left and walk along the pavement you will soon pass exit C.

Do not cross the road.

Continue straight ahead along the road you are on, 'Lok King Street'. Amongst other things you will be walking in the direction signposted 'Penfold Park' and 'Royal Ascot'.

0.45 **Continue straight ahead, crossing the road. Ignore the road going up to your left.** Your road is signposted 'Lok Shun Path'. Confusingly, the road to your left which you do not take is also signposted 'Lok Shun Path'.

Continue down to the large roundabout.

0.69 **Continue straight ahead, slightly to the left, following the pavement alongside the large main road which climbs steadily, (Figure 1).** Ignore the smaller road, also straight ahead, which runs down to the village and ignore the road sharply to your left.

Figure 1: Continue straight ahead along the pavement next to the large road.

0.90 **Turn left, leaving the pavement and taking the stairs which climb the hill straight ahead of you, (Figure 2).** Ignore the two paths going down to your left. The path you are on will bend around to the left after about 130m shortly after which there is a fork in the path.

Figure 2: Turn left, leaving the pavement and climbing the stairs.

1.03 **Take the right fork in the path** and follow the path upwards towards the right. You see luxury villas on the distant hill slope to your right.

1.31 ****ATTENTION** STOP at the top of the stairs when you see the green garbage depository on your right. Ahead of you is a road, to your left is a sign post labelled 'Ma Niu Village' and a lamp post. Take the SMALL DIRT TRACK starting IN BETWEEN the sign for Ma Niu Village and the lamp post, which goes steeply up the hill, (Figure 3).** DO NOT follow the road in either direction, if you are on a road you have gone the wrong way.

Figure 3: Take the path directly inbetween the sign and the lampost.

Continue along this path ignoring smaller offshoots. The path is overgrown.

1.35 **After 40m you will have a view of the racecourse to your left. Follow the path upwards to the right.** This path might be difficult to follow. Ignore the small mud path to the left.

Continue up the hill. As a guide, you should mainly be climbing with your back to the racecourse. You may lose the path occasionally, it is sometimes overgrown. Do not be tempted by any animal tracks going off to your right or left.

1.58 ****TRIG. STATION** Continue straight ahead, passing the trigonometrical station on your right - it is not marked on the Countryside Series map.** The path may change direction slightly but in general you must continue up the hill with your back to the racecourse.

1.71 **Continue up the hill, passing the open rock with the satellite dishes on it to your left.** The path continues to climb. It is still overgrown and still a mud path. Continue in same direction, as the path gets higher the foliage becomes slightly lower. Follow the undulating path until you reach the top of the climb.

2.40 **At the top of the first climb continue along your path towards Kau To Shan, (directly ahead of you).** Follow the main path as it bends towards the right to the trigonometrical station.

2.62 **TRIG. STATION** Turn left, walking down the hill, (Figure 4). This path goes quite steeply down the hill and may be overgrown in places. You will be travelling in the same general direction as before with your back to the racecourse. In the distance you can see a concrete road which is your next destination.

Figure 4: Turn left at the trigonometrical station, going down the hill.

WARNING Please be careful as sections of this path are steep, slippery and precarious.

The main path climbs up and down a few small hills, and occasionally changes direction slightly, but never for very long.

3.09 **ATTENTION** Continue up the hill towards the left at the clear junction. Do not take the path down the hill to the right.

3.37 Walk straight ahead onto the concrete road, just after passing the grass helicopter pad on your right.

Continue along the concrete road. You will pass a car parking space after about 240m.

4.04 Turn right, following the concrete road down the hill. Do not continue straight ahead.

SHORT CUT You can spare yourself the 6.99km walk through Tai Po Kau nature reserve and rejoin the hike at a later point. If you wish to take this shortcut then instead of turning right as described above, continue

Leave the concrete road and walk down the narrow stairs to your left.

straight ahead for about 450m. Now turn left, off the road, walking down the narrow stairs. There is a sign with its back to you at the stairs which has 'WB 14-1' written on the front. If you reach a large junction between three roads you have gone about 140m too far. Once on the stairs you can rejoin the hike at the **REJOIN AFTER SHORTCUT** section in the text on page 48.

4.15 Turn left off the road down the path signposted 'To Yellow and Brown Walk'. You will pass a map.

Turn right at the clear junction, walking up the small hill. You soon pass a sign labelled 'Brown Walk'.

4.45 Continue along the path, following it around to the right. Ignore the small path to your left with the 'Road Closed' sign in front of it.

5.73 Continue straight ahead along the Brown Walk, following the path slightly towards the left. Do not turn right along the Yellow Walk.

5.91 Continue straight ahead. Do not climb the steep hill leading to the Yellow Walk.

6.68 Turn left down the hill along the path signposted 'Nature Trail'. Do not turn right, signposted 'To Tai Po Road'.

6.89 Turn left along the Red and Blue Walk at the small intersection with the map. Do not continue straight ahead towards Tai Po Road. You will pass through a large picnic site and cross a bridge.

7.44 Turn left up the hill along the Blue Walk at the junction with the map. Do not continue straight ahead along the red walk.

8.11 ****ATTENTION**** At the next junction turn right along the Blue Walk and cross the river. Now take an IMMEDIATE left turn after crossing the bridge, **(Figure 5)**. Do not continue to your right along the Blue Walk and do not take the stairs up the hill just before you have crossed the small bridge.

Figure 5: Take the path immediately to your left after crossing the bridge.

WARNING This path is signposted as being 'Treacherous, Obscured or Seasonally Overgrown'. Please realise you continue AT YOUR OWN RISK.

8.18 Turn right up the hill, avoiding the path blocked by a 'Road Closed' sign.

9.09 Turn sharp left at the top of the hill, along the Yellow and Brown Walk along the clear mud path.

Continue straight ahead, along the Yellow and Brown Walk. Ignore the steps to your right labelled 'To Forest Track' after about 140m. You will pass a concrete water tank on your right and cross a few small streams. Ignore any minor, unsignposted paths going to your right or left.

10.42 **ATTENTION** You will pass a round yellow sign with a black border labelled WP 4-2 on your left. Turn right immediately, climbing the small narrow stairs labelled 'To Forest Track', (Figure 6). Do not continue straight ahead. If you pass a large boulder on your right, with a sign labelled 'Yellow and Brown walk', with a nearby path going down the hill then you have gone too far.

Figure 6: Turn right, climbing the narrow trail.

10.59 **ATTENTION** Take the second road on your left when you arrive at the road. Your direction is effectively straight ahead. Do not continue up the steep hill on your first left, which goes towards the fire lookout, and do not continue to your right.

As you follow the road round the first bend you see a yellow sign with a black border labelled 'WB 14-1'.

10.73 Turn right off the road down the concrete stairs directly next to the yellow sign labelled 'WB 14-1'. These stairs soon become stone.

REJOIN AFTER SHORTCUT If you decided to take the short cut then this is where you will rejoin the hike.

Continue along this path which soon becomes a mud path and crosses numerous small streams. It twists and turns. Do not be tempted by minor offshoots to the left or right. The path passes though woodland.

11.36 **ATTENTION** Upon exiting the woodland you have a clear, open view of the hills around you. Take the small mud path 90 degrees to your right climbing very steeply up the hill, (Figure 7). This path will eventually lead to the top of Grassy Hill, which you can locate on your map. The path is easy to miss. It is a very narrow, precarious mud path. There is a clear distinction between the woodland and the grass slope to your right. You need to look for the path as soon as you exit the woodland.

Figure 7: Climb the steep, narrow mud path, heading towards Grassy Hill.

Continue along this path up the hill.

11.65 ****ATTENTION**** When the first electricity pylon is directly to your right there is a small path leading to this pylon. DO NOT take this path but make a note of it and continue straight ahead.

Figure 8: Take the small, unclear path up the hill to the right.

11.78 130m from the pylon path there is a small, unclear, difficult to see mud path going up towards your right, (Figure 8). Take this path. The path is just before the grassy old stone wall (which may look like a grassy mound) on your right. If you pass this wall you have gone TOO FAR. DO NOT continue straight ahead slightly to the left.

Continue along the path. It climbs steeply, reaches the crest of the hill, bending slightly left. It then continues to run parallel to the woodland, which is about 20m away. You pass a large round boulder on your right after about 120m. The path undulates and there will be a steep drop.

12.13 **Cross the narrow stream** and begin the final ascent of Grassy Hill.

12.46 ****ATTENTION**** At the large cluster of rocks follow the path

up the hill directly to the right. You will pass the rocks closely on your right hand side. Do not continue straight ahead.

12.49 **Take the path to your right at the next small junction,** although you can take either path, as ultimately they both end up at the same place, as long as you are going up the hill.

Continue up Grassy Hill until you reach the concrete road.

12.88 **Follow the concrete road down the slope.** You will pass a **trigonometrical station** about 20m away to your right.

12.96 **Turn right, signposted 'Lead Mine Pass',** following the stairs down the hill. You are now on the MacLehose trail. Do not follow the concrete road to the left, down the hill.

13.53 **Turn left at the road,** passing a picnic site on your right.

Turn sharp right down the hill, continuing along the MacLehose trail, signposted 'Shing Mun Reservoir'. Do not continue straight ahead, signposted 'Needle Hill'. You will pass a helicopter pad on your left.

13.89 **Turn right off the road, continuing along the MacLehose trail,** just after passing the toilet on your right. You will pass through a picnic site and under a large sign labelled 'MacLehose Trail Stage 8'. Do not continue straight ahead down the hill along the road. Ignore the path going to your right signposted 'Tai Po'.

Continue up the hill along the steps.

WARNING The mud path you will now take contains many slippery rocks and you will cross several river beds and one large, wide stream. All these are potentially slippery and dangerous, especially when it is wet. Please consider this before continuing.

14.33 **Continue straight ahead up the hill at the junction, signposted 'Chuen Lung'.** Do not continue along the MacLehose trail to your right. The path you are on is a clear mud and rock path. Ignore any minor paths to your left or right.

15.80 **Take the mud path to your right at the junction between the two major mud paths.** The path you take continues steeply downhill to your right and you will soon pass a sign labelled 'Shing Mun

Reservoir' and 'Chuen Lung'. Do not take the mud path slightly to your left. You will cross a few small streams.

WARNING Crossing Tai Shing stream can potentially be very dangerous. Please beware of the slippery, dangerous boulders.

16.61 **Cross the large, wide stream VERY CAREFULLY. This is Tai Shing stream.**

Continue along the path on the other side of the stream which almost immediately crosses another small stream before bending to the left. Do not take the much smaller path up the hill to your right.

17.03 ****ATTENTION**** **Continue straight ahead, slightly towards the right, at the easy to miss junction. You are walking up some old stairs along the smaller of the two paths, (Figure 9).** Do not follow the wide main path steeply downhill towards the left. You will soon cross a few more smaller streams.

Figure 9: Continue straight ahead up the path slightly to your right.

18.14 **Continue straight ahead along the path signposted 'Shing Mun Reservoir'.** Ignore the path going to your right signposted 'Chuen Lung'.

18.92 **Continue straight ahead** at the bottom of the hill, signposted 'Shing Mun Reservoir'. Ignore the path to your right signposted 'Chuen Lung'. You will soon pass mileage post C3408 on your left.

19.04 **Continue straight ahead** along the Lung Mun country trail, signposted 'Shing Mun Reservoir'. Do not turn left, also signposted 'Shing Mun Reservoir'.

19.72 ****ATTENTION** Turn right at the road, continue for 4m, then turn left off the road down the stairs.**

Follow the path you are on, going down and passing through the picnic site.

Go down the stairs at the far right hand corner of the picnic site. The main picnic site will have been passed on your left.

19.86 | **Turn right** and follow the large, wide mud path near the reservoir. You will cross a small bridge to your left.

Continue along the mud path which soon follows a fence on your left hand side.

20.00 | **Continue down the concrete stairs slightly to your left** at the junction. You will pass the Shing Mun Reservoir Visitor Centre on your right hand side. Do not go slightly right up the hill.

The bus shelter immediately at the bottom of these stairs, on your left, signals the end of the hike. Up the hill to your right is the visitor centre where there are toilets and a public phone. A small kiosk is also sometimes open for refreshments.

20.16 | ****FINISH****

GETTING HOME Green mini bus 82 leaves from this bus shelter. This bus takes you to Tsuen Wan from where you can catch the MTR or another form of transport.

The mysterious bamboo groves on this hike offer some interesting textures.

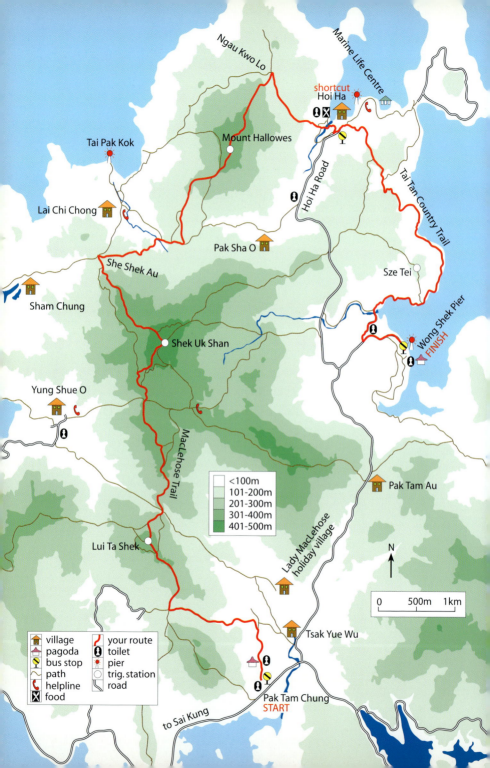

summary:

20.50km   7½h   Sai Kung & Clear Water Bay

starting point: 北潭涌

Pak Tam Chung

getting to start: from Sai Kung: 7 or 9 or 94 or $65 or 96R *

*96R Sundays & holidays only. This bus runs from Choi Hung MTR & Sai Kung.

Go to Sai Kung. Take green mini bus 7 (HK$10) or 9 (HK$5.5) or bus 94 (HK$5.5) or bus 96R, (Sundays and holidays only, HK$15.6) or a taxi (about HK$65) to Pak Tam Chung, which is not the terminus for any of these buses, so please ask where to get off. (More info. on getting to Sai Kung, Appendix, A-iii).

description:

The hike starts at Pak Tam Chung and heads up to Lui Ta Shek. It joins the MacLehose trail briefly then climbs Wa Mei Shan and Shek Uk Shan. We now go down to Nam Shan Tung before climbing Mount Hallowes and heading to Hoi Ha. The route then heads to the coast and on to Wong Shek Pier.

getting home: 94 or $90 or 96R * to Sai Kung

*96R Sundays & holidays only. This bus runs to Sai Kung & Choi Hung MTR.

Take bus 94 or a taxi (about HK$100) from Wong Shek to Sai Kung. On weekends and holidays bus 96R runs to Sai Kung and then on to Choi Hung MTR. There is an infrequent ferry from Wong Shek to Ma Liu Shui, which is close to University KCR station. (See main text).

WARNINGS:

Not recommended in wet weather. There are many steep climbs and descents during this hike. The descent from Lui Ta Shek is one of the steepest and most difficult in the book, although relatively short. Look out for the razor wire next to the fence at Shek Uk Shan, don't cut yourself.

hike Xsection:

GETTING TO START Go to Sai Kung and take green mini bus 7 (HK$10) or 9 (HK$5.5) or bus 94 (every day, HK$5.5) or 96R (Sundays and holidays only, HK$15.6) or a taxi (about HK$65) to Pak Tam Chung.

START

With your back to the road, walk past the 'Sai Kung Country Park Visitor Centre' on your right and continue straight ahead directly away from the road. You pass a toilet on your right hand side.

0.12 **Continue to the back right hand corner of the car park. Pass under the large arch labelled 'Pak Tam Chung', (Figure 1).** This also has 'Barbecue Site' and 'Family Walk' written on it.

0.23 **Turn left,** passing the toilet on your right hand side. Ignore the path up to the barbecue site and the steep concrete path going up towards your left.

Figure 1: Pass through the arch labelled 'Pak Tam Chung'.

0.78 **Turn left, signposted 'Tai Mong Tsai Road',** along the mud path. You will pass a path leading to a barbecue site on your right immediately afterwards. Do not continue straight ahead along the family walk, signposted 'Tsak Yue Wu'.

Continue along the main path, ignoring smaller paths to your left or right. You will cross a small stream after 1.09km.

2.12 ****ATTENTION**** At the small clearing, the intersection between 4 paths, take the unsignposted path immediately to your right, going up the hill, **(Figure 2).** This is the smallest of the 4 paths and is slightly overgrown at first but still easy to follow. It climbs towards Lui Ta Shek. Ignore the paths

Figure 2: Turn right up the hill, taking the smallest path.

straight ahead and to your left, signposted 'Tai Mong Tsai Road' and 'Tsam Chuk Wan' respectively.

Continue up the hill, which is steep, slippery and eroded.

2.70 **Continue straight ahead** up and over the small hill, ignoring the path to your left going around the hill.

3.02 **Continue straight ahead up the large hill, Lui Ta Shek.** Ignore the paths to your left and right which slant downhill.

WARNING The next path is one of the steepest, most technically difficult in this book. Please be careful.

3.20 ****TRIG. STATION** On Lui Ta Shek, turn right at the trigonometrical station, taking the small mud path going steeply down the hill.** Ignore the clearer path to your left.

After 70m the path bends around slightly to the left but continues down the hill. If the path becomes unclear just continue down the hill, ignoring paths to the left or right.

3.49 **Turn right, at the intersection with the wide, clear mud path.** You are now on the MacLehose trail. You will pass mileage post M060 on your left after about 30m.

3.72 **Take the second path to your left, signposted 'Cheung Sheung',** at the junction. You are continuing along the MacLehose trail. Ignore the paths directly to your left and to your right, labelled 'Yung Shue O' and 'Pak Tam Road' respectively.

Follow the main trail around to the right after 270m, do not climb the steep path. Ignore any other, smaller paths to your left or right, continuing along the MacLehose trail.

4.55 ****ATTENTION** Turn left at mileage post M058, walking steeply up the hill, (Figure 3).** You are leaving the MacLehose trail. Follow this path up the hill, do not take any smaller paths branching off it.

WARNING The next path passes close to some cliffs and

Figure 3: Turn left up the hill, leaving the MacLehose trail.

emerges at a warning sign. The path is very overgrown, so you will not see the cliffs, but please take care. YOU CONTINUE AT YOUR OWN RISK.

4.80   **Turn left** at the top of the second small climb, Wa Mei Shan. Your path will become slightly overgrown in places. Ignore the path to your right going back down to the MacLehose trail.

5.53   ****ATTENTION****   **Continue straight ahead up the hill along the clear mud path at the junction, (Figure 4).** Ignore the path crossing your route which is the 'Cheung Sheung Country Trail'.

Continue along the main path ignoring any minor offshoots to your right or left.

Figure 4: Continue straight ahead up the hill.

6.00   **Turn right onto the clear path leading up the hill.** Do not continue straight ahead down the hill on the path you were on.

6.48   **Continue straight ahead, climbing over the helicopter pad. You will be on a path running alongside the fence of the transmitting depot.** Do not take the path down to your right.

6.59   ****TRIG. STATION****   **Continue alongside the fence at Shek Uk Shan,** passing the trigonometrical station about 5m to your right.

Turn sharp left, going steeply down the hill, still walking alongside the fence.

Continue along the main path, ignoring any minor offshoots. Your path will leave the fence after about 60m, and then continue along the ridge of several hills before descending steeply down a slippery slope.

8.29   **Turn sharp right at the large, clear junction at the bottom of**

Figure 5: Turn sharp right and follow the path indicated by the arrows.

the eroded hill, **(Figure 5).** Your path is clear and gravelly. Ignore the path to your left and also the path slightly to your right going up the hill. You cross a couple of streams after about 340m.

9.24   **Cross the wide stream and continue straight ahead** up the stairs on the opposite bank.

9.31   **Turn right at the concrete path, signposted 'Pak Sha O'.** Ignore the path to your left signposted 'Lai Chi Chong'.

9.58   ****ATTENTION** About 270m after turning right you pass a dark green telephone post on your left hand side. About 40m after this post TURN LEFT along the steep mud path going up the hill, (Figure 6), leaving the concrete path.** If you reach a green telephone post on your right hand side then you have gone about 20m too far. DO NOT turn left up the small mud path which begins 5m after the green telephone post, this is very overgrown.

Figure 6: Turn left up the mud path beginning about 40m after the green post.

Continue up the hill along the narrow, overgrown path. It is always possible to follow.

10.13   **Turn right,** following the overgrown path up the hill at the small, unclear junction. Do not continue straight ahead towards the left.

10.53   **Continue straight ahead on the right hand side at the small clearing with the large rock.**

Continue up the hill along the main path. The path may branch in places but these branches usually rejoin each other soon afterwards.

11.40   ****TRIG. STATION** Continue straight ahead at Mount Hallowes, passing the trigonometrical station on your left.**

You pass through a small rock strewn area after about 640m, with your path going steeply downhill again soon afterwards. About 580m after the rocky area your path will become slightly hard to follow. Make sure you continue straight ahead.

12.80 **Turn right along the clear mud path at the clear junction between 4 narrow mud paths.** Ignore the path going sharply to your left and also that leading straight ahead.

You pass through a small, mysterious woodland after about 260m, with your path bending slightly left and then right again, crossing a very narrow stream. About 480m after the woodland the main path becomes very rocky as it heads downhill.

14.13 **Turn right, crossing the wide stream at the bottom of the hill.** Ignore the path going to your left through a small bamboo grove.

14.14 **Turn left immediately after crossing the stream,** following the path through the campsite and around to the right as it hugs the coast. The path will soon become concrete after about 210m and then soon climbs up to a road.

14.41 **Turn left at the large, tarmaced road,** next to the telephone box.

14.48 **You reach the entrance to Hoi Ha village.**

SHORT CUT If you are tired at this point of the hike you can end the hike here at Hoi Ha. Green mini bus 7 (HK$10) to Sai Kung leaves from the large turning area just before entering the village. A taxi to Sai Kung costs about HK$100.

14.48 **Continue straight ahead slightly to the left, signposted 'Wan Tsai Campsites'.** You are now on a concrete road. Ignore the concrete driveway to your right.

14.55 **Turn right, following the main concrete road/path.**

About 20m after turning right follow the path around to the left.

After about 10m, turn right. The path will now pass several restaurants on your right hand side.

FOOD If you're hungry or need to stock up on refreshments, then now is the time.

14.71 ****ATTENTION** Soon after passing the restaurants, there is a signpost on your left labelled 'Tai Tan' and 'Wan Tsai'. STOP here and TURN RIGHT up the wide, rocky path,** (Figure 7). You are leaving the main, paved path which bends around to the left towards the coast.

Figure 7: Turn right up the wide, rocky path.

15.48 Continue along the path you are on, ignoring any smaller paths to your left or right. You will pass a trigonometrical station about 5m to your left after about 290m. The path is now a mud path.

15.68 **Continue straight ahead slightly towards the left** at the small junction. Ignore the path going sharply to your right.

15.76 **Continue straight ahead** along the path you are on, ignoring the path which climbs steeply to your left.

15.83 **Continue straight ahead towards the right, steeply down the hill.** Ignore the clear mud path towards the left. You will cross a stream after about 50m, before bending around to the left and joining a wide hiking trail.

15.98 **Turn right at the clear, wide hiking trail.** You are now on the 'Tai Tan Country Trail'. The trail will almost immediately start climbing a small hill.

17.05 **Turn left at the junction, signposted 'Tai Tan'.** You will pass a map on your right. Ignore the small mud path to your right. You will pass mileage post C5408 after about 100m.

18.99 **Continue straight ahead along the beach,** rejoining the path on the other side.

19.01 **Continue straight ahead at the village,** passing the houses on your right.

19.17 ****ATTENTION** Turn right after the second village house, about 20m after arriving at the houses. Your path passes between 2 village houses,** (Figure 8). About 10m after turning right your path bends around to the left.

19.20 Follow the concrete path down the hill, ignoring the path going up to your right. You will cross a bridge after about 30m.

Continue along the road. Ignore any paths branching off from it.

Figure 8: Turn right after passing the second village house.

19.66 Turn left at the large, tarmaced road. You will now follow this road for about 840m all the way to Wong Shek Pier.

20.50 **FINISH**

GETTING HOME Take bus 94 (every day) or 96R (Sundays & holidays only) or a taxi (about HK$90) from Wong Shek Pier to Sai Kung. There is also a ferry from Wong Shek to Ma Liu Shui, near University KCR. This ferry leaves at 10.35 and 16.55.

An old village house hides in the lush greenery near Chek Keng village, hike 10.

The paths around Plover Cove Reservoir, hike 7, are steep, slippery and technical.

Hike 7: Tai Mei Tuk round trip

summary:

| | 26.10km | 8½h | North East & Central NT | | |

starting point: 大尾篤總站

Tai Mei Tuk

getting to start: Tai Po Market + 20C or 75K or $60

Take the KCR to Tai Po Market KCR station. Take green mini bus 20C (HK$6), bus 75K (HK$4.7) or a green taxi (about HK$60) to Tai Mei Tuk. (More info. Appendix A-iii).

description:

The hike starts at Tai Mei Tuk and follows the Pat Sin Leng nature trail to Bride's pool. It then brushes past Wu Kau Tang before climbing to the ridge above Plover Cove reservoir. From here the hike generally continues around the reservoir with a couple of unexpected detours along the way. We finish off at the main dam, which heads back to Tai Mei Tuk.

getting home: 20C or 75K or $60 + Tai Po Market

Take green mini bus 20C (HK$6), bus 75K (HK$4.7) or a taxi (about HK$60) to Tai Po Market KCR station.

WARNINGS:

This hike will be precarious and slippery in the wet. You also need to be aware of long exposure to the sun and steep, relentless, gravelly climbs and descents.

hike Xsection:

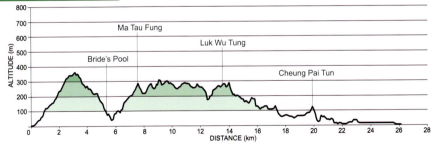

GETTING TO START Take the KCR to Tai Po Market station. Take green mini bus 20C (HK$6), bus 75K (HK$4.7) or a taxi (about HK$60) to Tai Mei Tuk.

START

From the bus stop or taxi rank, face the main, tarmaced road along which you just arrived.

Walk to this main, tarmaced road and turn right, following the road. Ignore any turnings to your left or right. You are walking in the direction of the Pat Sin Leng nature trail.

0.67 At the top of the hill leave the tarmaced road and follow the smaller, concrete road up the hill slightly towards your left, signposted 'Pat Sin Leng Nature Trail', (Figure 1). You will have passed the visitor centre driveway on your left just before leaving the road and the 'Agriculture, Fisheries and Conservation Department, Plover Cove Country Park, Tai Mei Tuk Management Centre' sign to your right. The path bends to the left up the hill. Do not follow 'Bride's Pool Road' down the hill.

Figure 1: Leave the main road, heading up towards the nature trail.

0.76 Turn right, crossing the concrete bridge with the blue railings. You will pass under a sign labelled 'Pat Sin Leng Nature Trail'. Do not continue along the road up the hill.

Continue up the steps along the nature trail. You will pass through the 'Spring Breeze Pavilion Memorial' after about 100m and also pass regular numbered nature trail posts.

ATTENTION The hike now follows the Pat Sin Leng nature trail all the way to Bride's Pool Road. If you do not need more detailed instructions than this skip straight to the **BRIDE'S POOL ROAD** section.

1.05 Ignore the steep path to your left marked with 'Danger' and 'Warning' signs.

1.72 Continue along the nature trail, signposted 'Wan Shan Keuk'.

Ignore the path to your right labelled 'Bride's Pool Road'.

2.71 **Continue along the main path, which bends to the left,** at the junction with the emergency helpline. This is signposted 'Bride's Pool' and you are now on the Wilson trail. Do not go sharply left up the hill to Pat Sin Leng. Ignore the small mud path to your right.

2.86 Cross the stream, following the path around to the right. You will soon pass nature trail post number 15 and Wilson trail mileage post W127.

3.53 Continue along the nature trail after crossing the narrow stream near post W128.

3.75 Cross the wide stream, following the path around to the right.

4.06 **Continue straight ahead, slightly to the right at the junction, signposted 'Bride's Pool'.** Do not turn left along the Wilson trail, signposted 'Luk Keng'.

4.45 **Cross the stream and continue up the steps towards the left** along the nature trail. Do not follow any mud paths just before crossing the stream or the path to your right just after crossing the stream.

4.60 **Continue along the main path, signposted 'Bride's Pool'.** Ignore the mud path to your left.

BRIDE'S POOL ROAD

5.35 **Cross the road and pass under the large sign to your left labelled 'Bride's Pool Nature Trail'.** You will pass a map on your left.

Continue down the stairs, crossing the bridge and passing through the picnic site.

5.43 **Follow the path to the right, signposted 'Chung Mei' and 'Wu Kau Tang'.** Ignore any smaller paths branching off it.

5.74 **Cross the concrete bridge with the brown railings,** which bends around to your right. Do not climb the concrete steps found just before the bridge on your left, signposted 'Bride's Pool'.

5.76 **Follow the trail up the hill slightly to your left** immediately after crossing the bridge, signposted 'Chung Mei'. You pass a map on your left. Ignore the picnic site to your right.

5.82 **Turn sharp left up the stairs,** along the mud path signposted 'Wu Kau Tang'. Do not continue straight ahead to Chung Mei. These stairs twist and turn and continue up the hill.

5.92 **Turn left towards 'Wu Kau Tang' at the junction.** Ignore the path towards 'Chung Mei'.

Continue along the main, stony path. Ignore the clear stairs to your right after about 300m.

6.32 ****ATTENTION** Turn right along the small mud path climbing steeply up the hill, which starts from DIRECTLY INBETWEEN the stone signpost and the lamp post, (Figure 2).** The signpost is labelled 'Sam A Tsuen' and 'Sam A Chung'. The signpost is found just after passing a small altar on your right and a bridge on your left. If you reach the small concrete path to your right or the second bridge straight ahead, you have gone too far.

Figure 2: The path starts from between the stone sign and the lamp post.

Continue up the hill along the main, clearly visible mud path, ignoring any smaller paths.

6.66 **Turn left at the top of the hill,** along the clear mud path. You have an open view of the reservoir from here.

Continue along the clear mud path, up and down various small hills.

7.61 ****TRIG. STATION** Continue straight ahead along the main mud path at Ma Tau Fung.** The path will twist and turn and rise and fall.

9.14 ****TRIG. STATION** Continue straight ahead along the main path.**

9.63 **Turn right at the clear junction** with a wide mud path. Ignore the path to your left.

WARNING Please be careful on the next path as there are some steep drops to your right.

10.68 Turn right again at the next clear junction with a mud path, once again ignoring the path to your left.

11.81 Continue along your main path at Mount Newland. Ignore the small path to your left.

12.53 Continue down the steps into the denser shrubbery, after which your path starts to climb steeply. Ignore any smaller paths to the left or right.

13.54 **ATTENTION** Continue straight ahead, slightly to the left, along the slightly overgrown path at Luk Wu Tung, (Figure 3). DO NOT turn sharply to your right onto the path going steeply down the hill.

Continue along your path. You should see a peak with a trigonometrical station you will eventually pass in the distance.

Figure 3: Continue straight ahead along the narrow, hard to see path.

14.02 **TRIG. STATION** Continue straight ahead down the hill.

14.10 **WARNING** Make sure you follow the path round to the right at the large boulder, there is a steep drop straight ahead. The path then turns left again continuing down the hill.

14.36 **ATTENTION** About 260m after the big boulder turn right at the minor junction between two unclear paths, (Figure 4). Do not end up walking to your left.

Figure 4: Turn right at the small, unclear junction.

14.44 **ATTENTION** About 80m after the last junction, turn sharply right along the very overgrown, narrow mud path, (Figure 5). This path is extremely hard to find. It begins near the bottom of the small hill, just before the clear main path bends around to the left.

Continue along the mud path which is overgrown yet easy to

follow. Ignore any even smaller paths branching off from it.
You will be heading back in
the general direction you came
from.

15.05 Pass through the tiny woodland, continuing in the same direction.

15.34 Pass through the next woodland, continuing in the same direction. You will soon reach a junction with a clear mud path.

Figure 5: Turn sharp right along the narrow, extremely overgrown path.

15.39 **Turn left at the clear mud path.** You will see the reservoir on your right again after about 150m.

WARNING The are some steep and tricky decents between now and the end of the hike, please be careful.

15.73 **Follow the wide main mud path to your right,** down the steep hill at Ngor Kai Teng. Ignore the smaller path straight ahead.

Continue along the main, easy to follow mud path. Ignore any smaller, less distinct paths branching off from it. It will climb and fall significantly.

19.89 ****TRIG. STATION** Continue straight ahead and down the hill at Cheung Pai Tun.** Follow the main path as it undulates and bends towards the left.

20.51 **Follow the path around to the right at the top of the small hill.** Ignore the path going down to your left. You will eventually reach some steps going down to a small dam.

21.44 **Turn right,** walking along the wide concrete path alongside the small dam.

21.62 **Follow the road round slightly to the left.** Ignore the stairs with the blue railings.

21.67 **Turn right,** climbing the stairs.

21.69 **Turn left** along the raised path with the blue railings.

21.93 **Turn left down the stairs and follow the large road, round to the right.**

Continue along the road, passing the waterworks buildings and ignoring any smaller, minor roads.

23.57 | **Turn right onto the main dam.**

Cross the painfully long main dam.

25.57 | **Follow the road around to the left after crossing the dam,** passing the helicopter pad on your right. You will pass a small traffic island on your left after about 230m.

25.97 | **Continue along the pavement,** following it around to the right and passing the small shop on your left.

Continue in the same direction.

You have arrived at Tai Mei Tuk, with the bus stops and taxi rank to your left.

26.10 | ****FINISH****

GETTING HOME The bus stop and taxi rank are directly ahead of you. You can either take bus number 75K (HK$4.7), green mini bus number 20C (HK$6) or a taxi (about HK$60) to Tai Po Market KCR station.

The 2km main dam of Plover Cover Reservoir can seem painfully long at times.

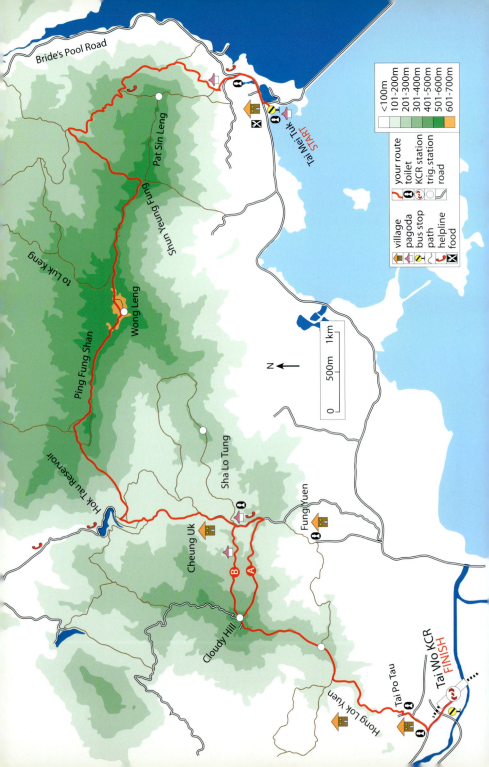

HIKE 8: Tai Mei Tuk to Tai Wo KCR via Ping Fung Shan

summary:

starting point: 大尾篤總站

Tai Mei Tuk

getting to start: Tai Po Market + 20C or 75K or $60

Take the KCR to Tai Po Market KCR station. Take green mini bus 20C (HK$6), bus 75K (HK$4.7) or a green taxi (about HK$60) to Tai Mei Tuk. (More info. Appendix A-iii).

description:

The hike starts at Tai Mei Tuk and follows the Pat Sin Leng family walk for a short while before taking a difficult path up to the ridge near Shun Yeung Fung. We then follow the ridge and descend close to Hoi Ha Reservoir before climbing Cloudy Hill along an overgrown, narrow path and heading down to Tai Wo KCR station.

getting home: Tai Wo

Take the KCR from Tai Wo station.

WARNINGS:

Not recommended in wet weather. Some paths on this hike are difficult to find as well as overgrown. Many of the paths are overgrown with ferns which can leave nasty scratches on legs and arms so long trousers and sleeves might be a good idea. The last climb up to Cloudy Hill is particularly overgrown and one of the most technically difficult of all those in this book. An easier alternative is suggested.

hike Xsection:

km from start	

GETTING TO START Take the KCR to Tai Po Market station. Take green mini bus 20C (HK$6), bus 75K (HK$4.7) or a taxi (about HK$60) to Tai Mei Tuk.

START

From the bus stop or taxi rank, face the main, tarmaced road along which you just arrived.

Walk to this main, tarmaced road and turn right, following the road. Ignore any turnings to your left or right. You are walking in the direction of the Pat Sin Leng nature trail.

0.67 — **At the top of the hill leave the tarmaced road and follow the smaller, concrete road up the hill slightly towards your left, signposted 'Pat Sin Leng Nature Trail',** (**Figure 1**). You will have passed the visitor centre driveway on your left just before leaving the road and the 'Agriculture, Fisheries and Conservation Department, Plover Cove Country Park, Tai Mei Tuk Management Centre' sign on your right. The path bends to the left up the hill. Do not follow 'Bride's Pool Road' down the hill.

Figure 1: Leave the main road, heading up towards the nature trail.

0.76 — **Turn right, crossing the concrete bridge** with the blue railings. You will pass under a sign labelled 'Pat Sin Leng Nature Trail'. Do not continue along the road up the hill.

Continue up the steps along the nature trail. You will pass through the 'Spring Breeze Pavilion Memorial' after about 100m and also pass regular numbered nature trail posts.

1.05 — **Ignore the steep path to your left marked with 'Danger' and 'Warning' signs.**

1.72 — **Continue along the nature trail, signposted 'Wan Shan Keuk'.** Ignore the path to your right labelled 'Bride's Pool Road'.

2.71 — **Continue along the main path, which bends to the left,** at the junction with the **emergency helpline.** This is signposted 'Bride's Pool' and you are now on the Wilson trail. Do not go sharply left up the hill to Pat Sin Leng. Ignore the small mud path to your right.

2.86 Cross the stream, following the path around to the right. You will soon pass nature trail post number 15 and Wilson trail mileage post W127.

3.53 Continue along the nature trail after crossing the narrow stream near post W128.

3.75 Cross the wide stream, following the path around to the right.

WARNING The next path is steep, narrow and extremely slippery in places.

3.81 ****ATTENTION** Please take note of when you pass nature trail mileage post 19 on your left.**

3.98 ****ATTENTION** About 170m after mileage post 19 there is a nature trail post with NO NUMBER, only a white bird above a white flower. Take the path going up the hill to your left, DIRECTLY NEXT TO this post, (Figure 2).** If you reach nature trail post number 20 you have gone too far. This path is narrow and extremely overgrown, but it is always possible to follow or guess the direction it is heading in. As a general rule, if you have a choice between paths always select the path heading upwards. After about 660m the path descends a slippery mud slope.

Figure 2: Take the path up the hill from directly next to the nature trail post.

4.65 ****ATTENTION** Turn right steeply up the hill just after the steep down slope, (Figure 3).** Do not take the mud path going straight ahead down the hill. The path you are on undulates slightly, but in general climbs steeply through thick shrubbery. You begin your final ascent up

Figure 3: Take the path going steeply up the hill to your right.

to the ridge close to Shun Yeung Fung about 580m after turning right.

5.32 **Turn right along the clear mud path, the Wilson Trail, after reaching the open ridge at the top of the hill.** There is a signpost a few metres to your left which you can look at if you wish. Your path to the right is labelled 'Hok Tau'. As you continue down the concrete stairs you will pass another sign after about 70m and distance post W123 about 220m after this sign.

6.61 **Continue up the stone stairs towards your left** at the junction next to distance post W121. Ignore the clearer path that heads slightly towards the right.

7.01 **Continue straight ahead slightly towards the left** at the junction just after passing distance post W120. This is signposted 'Hok Tau'. Do not go sharply right signposted 'Bride's Pool and Wang Shan Keuk'.

7.18 **Continue straight ahead** at the next signpost, labelled 'Hok Tau'.

7.59 **Continue along the main path** going down the hill, passing mileage post W119 on your left. Do not take the small mud path up the hill.

7.90 **Continue around the hill** on the path slightly to your right. Do not go directly over the hill.

WARNING There are steep cliffs in this area, so please take extreme caution, heed the danger signs and stay on the path.

8.82 **Continue straight ahead, signposted 'Hok Tau'.** Do not go right towards 'Tan Chuk Hang'. You will cross a small bridge after about 200m and pass distance post W116 about 110m after the bridge.

9.62 **Continue straight ahead down the hill, signposted 'Hok Tau'.** Do not take the small path to your right.

10.26 **Turn right at the large junction at the bottom of the hill, signposted 'Hok Tau'.** Do not turn left, signposted 'Ping Shan Chai'.

10.43 **Turn left off the main path, along the clear mud path next to**

the bin.

Continue straight ahead through the picnic site, ignoring any smaller paths to your right or to your left.

10.59 **ATTENTION** Take the small mud path down the hill at the back left hand corner of the picnic site, (Figure 4). This path is not clearly visible.

10.70 **Turn left at the large, wide mud path.** You will cross two bridges and the path will wind as it climbs a small hill.

10.87 **Turn left at the junction, signposted 'Sha Lo Tung'.** Do not turn right, signposted 'Hok Tau Reservoir'.

11.63 **Cross the wide stream over the concrete dam** as the path bends around to the left, continuing along your path on the other side.

Figure 4: Take the small mud path down the hill at the back of the picnic site.

11.68 **Turn right along the old, broken concrete path, towards 'Fung Yuen'.** Do not turn left towards 'Ping Shan Chai' or take the mud road straight ahead.

11.80 **Turn left up the mud road** just after the path has bent around to the right. Do not continue straight ahead towards Cheung Uk village along the narrow path. At this junction you are about 150m from the village.

12.05 **Follow the mud road around to the right, just after passing an isolated building on your right hand side.** Do not take any smaller paths leading off to your left or right. You will pass some graves on your right after 100m. The road is now broken up concrete.

12.27 **ATTENTION** STOP at the path going sharply up towards your right, signposted 'Cloudy Hill', and read what is below.

There are now two options to continue your hike:

ROUTE A, is the HKhiking.com path. This is one of the most overgrown, treacherous and difficult paths in this book, and eventually ends up at the top of Cloudy Hill. Only proceed if you are an experienced hiker ready for a challenge. Long trousers are recommended. Do not take this path if you are with a large, potentially slow group.

ROUTE B is an easy climb. It follows a clear path which also ends up at the top of Cloudy Hill. If you wish to take this route go directly to the **ROUTE B** heading on page 79.

ATTENTION If your group decides to split up into easy and hard categories you can meet at the top of Cloudy Hill, next to the silver map labelled 'Wilson Trail'.

ROUTE A - DIFFICULT

12.27 **Continue straight ahead at the signpost.** Ignore the path going up to your right labelled 'Cloudy Hill'. You will cross a concrete bridge.

Follow the concrete road around to the right, you will pass a shelter, an **emergency helpline** and a toilet on your left hand side. Soon afterwards you will pass a ramshackle house on your right hand side.

12.71 **ATTENTION** **Just past the top of a small incline there is a large telephone post on your right. Turn right, along the small mud path which begins about 3m BEFORE you reach the post,** (Figure 5). This path climbs steeply up the hill. Do not continue straight ahead along the concrete road.

Figure 5: Go steeply up the hill to your right, 3m before the telephone post.

12.75 **Turn right at the top of the first steep climb and then follow the path around to the left again soon afterwards.** It then generally continues straight ahead along the ridge of the hill, climbing continuously towards Cloudy Hill. You will probably need to push your way through dense undergrowth in places. Try to remember your general direction towards the top of Cloudy Hill.

13.72 **Turn 90 degrees to your right, continuing steeply up the hill at**

the tiny, overgrown junction just past the thick bamboo grove. The path continues to climb steeply.

13.81 **If you have a choice, always take the path going up the hill as opposed to any other.** You can clearly see the transmitting station at the top of Cloudy Hill straight ahead of you.

13.93 **Continue up the hill slightly towards the right.** This path is extremely overgrown and there is a small, clearer path straight ahead which you should not take.

14.16 ****WARNING** Look out for the roughly 50cm wide deep, eroded ridge running directly across your path. This is potentially very dangerous and may be overgrown and well hidden.**

14.38 ****TRIG. STATION** On Cloudy Hill turn left,** following the mud path down the hill. Ignore the steps going down to your right.

14.43 **Turn left at the concrete road.**

14.46 **Turn left, along the narrow concrete path.** Do not continue along the road.

14.48 ****ATTENTION**** If some of your group are doing **ROUTE B,** STOP at the silver map on your left hand side labelled 'Wilson Trail'. This is where you will meet up with the people doing the easy route.

A description of ****ROUTE B****, the easy route, now follows. The hike will continue from the section headed ****FROM CLOUDY HILL**** on **page 80**

****ROUTE B - EASY****

Turn right up the path signposted 'Cloudy Hill'. You will now follow the clear, main path up the hill up some steps.

Turn right down the concrete path near the top of Cloudy Hill.

Turn left at the road, ignoring the road to your right signposted 'Lau Shui Heung Reservoir'.

Take the narrow concrete path to your left. Do not continue along the road.

ATTENTION If some of your group are doing the difficult route, STOP at the silver map on your left hand side labelled 'Wilson Trail'. This is where you will meet up with the people doing the difficult route.

FROM CLOUDY HILL

14.48 **Continue straight ahead from next to the map,** following the concrete path down the hill. You are now on the Wilson trail again. The main path undulates up and down a few hills. Ignore any smaller paths to your left or right.

15.64 **TRIG. STATION** **Continue straight ahead** along the main path, ignoring smaller paths to your left or right.

16.13 **Turn left, signposted 'Tai Po Tau Village',** staying on the main path. Do not go right towards the benches.

16.37 **Follow the main path towards the left** just after mileage post W101, continuing down the hill. The path becomes green with a reddish brown border. Continue in the direction of 'Tai Po Tau Village' at the signpost. You will pass a couple of pagodas.

17.48 **Turn left along the concrete path at the village.** Your path runs alongside a broken up concrete road.

17.53 **Turn right at the clear, large road.** There is a signpost labelled 'Tai Po Tau'. You will pass a toilet and mileage post W99 to your left.

17.59 **Continue straight ahead along the road you are on, signposted 'Tai Po Tau Drive',** ignoring 'Tai Po Tau Road' to your left. You can walk along the path next to the village houses on your right if you want more tranquility.

17.82 **Turn right along the small side road, signposted 'Subway'.** Ignore the road you were on as it bends around to the left.

17.85 **Turn left, going through the subway, signposted 'Wilson Trail'.**

17.88 **Turn left** along the pavement next to the main road.

18.15 **Continue straight ahead at the large intersection, crossing the large road ahead of you. Make sure you stay on the same side of the road.** There are no pedestrian lights straight ahead so you will need to cross the road to your right, then cross to your left and then cross to your left again in order to end up on the other side of the road ahead of you.

18.24	**Continue straight ahead,** walking alongside 'Po Nga Road'.
18.46	**Go up the escalator directly ahead of you as you reach the bus depot on your right.**
18.51	**Turn right** at the top of the escalator.
	Tai Wo KCR station is now on your left hand side.
18.55	****FINISH****
	GETTING HOME Take the KCR from Tai Wo KCR station.

The tranquil village square at Lai Chi Wo, hike 9, with the ancient banyan tree.

Legend:
- your route
- toilet
- pier
- trig. station
- road
- temple
- village
- pagoda
- bus stop
- path
- helpline
- food

Sam A Tsuen

Kop Tong

Tiu Tang Lung

Wu Kau Tang

Lai Chi Wo

Mui Tsz Lam

So Lo Pun

Yung Shue Au

Kuk Po

Fung Hang

Bride's Pool Road

CHINA

Sha Tau Kok Road

START/FINISH
Luk Keng

Nam Chung

N

1km
500m
0

Elevation:
- <100m
- 101-200m
- 201-300m
- 301-400m
- 401-500m
- 501-600m

HIKE 9: Luk Keng round trip

summary:

	20.50km	8h	North East & Central NT			

starting point: 鹿頸

Luk Keng

getting to start: Fanling + 56K or $90

Take the KCR to Fanling station. Take green mini bus 56K (HK$7) or a green taxi (about HK$90) to Luk Keng. Please make sure your bus does actually go to Luk Keng, as some buses with the same number (56K) go to different destinations. (More info. Appendix, A-iv).

description:

The hike starts at Luk Keng and then climbs the family trail before taking a series of paths to the top of Tiu Tang Lung. It then goes down to Kop Tong, passes close to Mui Tsz Lam and heads to Lai Chi Wo. From here the path heads to So Lo Pun before taking an undulating route to Kuk Po from where it generally follows the coast all the way back to Luk Keng.

getting home: 56K or $90 + Fanling

Take green mini bus 56K or a green taxi (about HK$90) from Luk Keng to Fanling KCR station.

WARNINGS:

This hike is not recommended in wet weather. It contains numerous muddy, slippery climbs and descents as well as probably the most technically difficult descent in this book, down a steep, muddy, slippery, moss covered rock strewn path. This descent earns the hike a Flying Bottle rating.

hike Xsection:

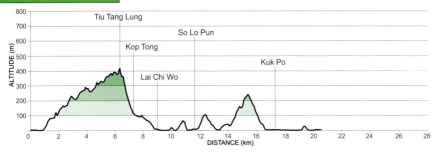

GETTING TO START Take the KCR to Fanling station. Take green mini bus 56K (HK$7) or a taxi (about HK$90) to Luk Keng.

START

Walk down wide, tarmaced 'Bride's Pool Road', which is on your left with respect to the road you just arrived on, which is 'Luk Keng Road'. You almost immediately cross a bridge and will pass a pagoda and car park on your left after about 110m.

0.28 **Turn left off the road,** walking along the concrete side road signposted 'Kai Kuk Shue Ha'. You will pass a sign labelled 'Fung Hang Family Walk' on your right. Do not continue along the larger road which bends around to the right.

0.41 **Follow the road around to the left,** it soon becomes a mud path and then a concrete path. Ignore the path to your right leading to the main village.

0.87 **Turn right and climb up the hill** at the junction with the **emergency helpline.** You pass through a sign with Chinese characters on it. Do not continue along the path signposted 'Lai Chi Wo' and 'Yung Shue Au'.

1.41 **Continue straight ahead.** Ignore the path sharply to your right, which leads to the compass, and any other smaller paths to the left or right. You will pass a picnic site on your right.

1.67 ****ATTENTION**** **Immediately after the picnic site continue straight ahead along the narrow path climbing steeply up the hill, (Figure 1). DO NOT continue along the family walk down the hill to your right.** Your path undulates steeply up and down a few hills and may be overgrown in places. Ignore any smaller paths leading off to the left or right.

Figure 1: Continue straight ahead, steeply up the hill.

3.44 **Turn left at the small junction at the top of the hill after the bamboo grove.** Ignore the path to your right which goes down the hill.

3.48 **Continue straight ahead, slightly to the left** at the large wide mud path. This is signposted 'Wu Kau Tang' after about 60m. You will soon pass distance post C2403 on your right hand side.

3.96 ****TRIG. STATION** Continue straight ahead slightly to the left,** down the hill. You will pass the fire lookout and trigonometrical station on your right hand side.

4.15 **Turn left signposted 'Lai Chi Wo' and 'Kuk Po',** along the wide mud path. Ignore the path to your right, signposted 'Wu Kau Tang'.

WARNING The next footpath is overgrown, slippery, and extremely steep, and is not recommended in wet weather. Please realise you CONTINUE AT YOUR OWN RISK.

4.26 ****ATTENTION** 110m after the last junction turn right along the small, well hidden path,** (Figure 2). You are leaving the main path, which continues down the hill. **There is a warning sign labelled 'The Path Ahead Is Treacherous, Obscured or Seasonally Overgrown', please heed this warning.**

Figure 2: Turn right along the well hidden path with the warning sign.

Always continue along the clearest path. Ignore the path to your left after about 10m. You will go left, steeply downhill after about 220m and pass through a hollow after about 250m before climbing very steeply out of it and heading towards Tiu Tang Lung.

5.21 **Turn left up the hill** at the clear junction with the narrow, rocky mud path. Ignore the path going steeply downhill to your right.

Continue up the hill. Ignore any paths going downhill.

6.29 ****TRIG. STATION** At the top of Tiu Tang Lung continue in the same direction,** passing the trigonometrical station on your right and continuing down the hill slightly to the left.

Turn left after 30 metres at the small junction, ignoring the path that goes towards the right.

WARNING The path that follows is one of the most difficult in this book. It is steep, slippery, covered in precarious rocks and sharp drops. It should not be attempted in wet weather.

6.44   ****ATTENTION** Turn left down the hill along the small, overgrown path 130m after the trigonometrical station, (Figure 3).** Ignore the main path which bends slightly towards the right, straight ahead of you.

Figure 3: This path is steep, narrow and technical.

Continue down this path all the way to Kop Tong village. As a general rule ignore any paths to your left and always follow the widest path which continues downwards, very steeply in places. This path may occasionally be hard to find. As general guides, after about 560m you will cross a river bed to your right and then follow the path down towards the left. About 110m after this you will pass a sunken concrete well on your left hand side and about 250m after this the path drops steeply, turns 90 degrees to the left, and runs alongside a stream on your right until you are almost at Kop Tong village.

7.28   **At Kop Tong village, continue along the concrete path down the hill.** You pass the village on your left hand side. Do not turn into the village.

7.36   **Turn left, signposted 'Mui Tsz Lam',** walking along the concrete path. Do not walk straight ahead towards 'Lai Chi Wo' and 'Sam A Tsuen'.

7.83   ****ATTENTION** After crossing the stream, climb the 7 steps and continue straight ahead, slightly to the right, along the muddy, grassy path, (Figure 4).** DO NOT follow the concrete path to your left which leads to Mui Tsz Lam.

7.91   **Turn right at the concrete path.**

Figure 4: Follow the grassy path straight ahead slightly to the right.

This path leads towards Lai Chi Wo, and basically continues in the same direction as the mud path.

8.81 **Turn left, signposted 'Lai Chi Wo',** at the junction between concrete paths found shortly after crossing the bridge. **You will cross a stream.** Do not continue straight ahead, signposted 'Sam A Tsuen'.

8.93 **Continue straight ahead, signposted 'Lai Chi Wo',** walking through the large gate with Chinese writing on it. Ignore the path to your left signposted 'Lai Chi Wo Fung Shui Woodland' and 'Fang Shui Au'.

8.93 **Continue straight ahead slightly to the right** along the narrow path which runs directly next to the wall. Ignore the wider path leading slightly to the left.

9.01 **Turn right through the next large gate.** The concrete path bends around to the left before bending to the right past a **public toilet** and heading down to **Lai Chi Wo village square.**

9.07 **Turn left at the village square and walk straight ahead to the corner which is now directly ahead of you.** You will pass the village houses closely to your left.

9.13 **Continue straight ahead** along the concrete path. You will pass the 'Lai Chi Wo Tourist Map' on your left hand side and a large beige building on your right hand side. After about 190m your path bends to the left and follows the coast.

9.50 **Continue along the main concrete path which passes a pier on your right hand side and is signposted 'So Lo Pun', 'Yung Shue Au' and 'Kuk Po'.** After about 370m the path climbs slightly to your left, leaving the coast. It soon becomes a mud path. Ignore the concrete path to your right about 200m after this and any other smaller paths. The path will eventually go back down to the coast before once again leaving it to your left.

10.82 **Continue up the hill towards the right, signposted 'So Lo Pun'.** The path will soon bend down to the left. Ignore the small mud path going down the hill straight ahead of you.

11.06 **Continue along the concrete path next to the coast,** with the sea to your right.

11.21 **Turn left, signposted 'So Lo Pun'.** You are once again turning away from the coast. Ignore the path to your right.

11.61 **Continue along the main path through So Lo Pun village.** Ignore minor paths to your left or right.

11.84 Continue straight ahead along the main path, signposted using a yellow arrow and a tree. Ignore the concrete path to your left.

11.94 **Turn right up the hill, signposted 'Yung Shue Au'.** Ingore the path leading straight ahead. Ignore any paths leading to the left or right off the main path you are now on.

13.09 Continue along the path, passing the signpost for 'Yung Shue Au'.

13.26 **At Yung Shue Au village continue along the concrete path,** passing the village houses closely to your left.

13.41 **Turn left up the small path signposted 'Ah Kung Au'.** Ignore the main path which continues straight ahead. Your path soon becomes a concrete path which passes through old village houses.

14.17 **Continue straight ahead, signposted 'Kuk Po',** walking up the stone stairs. Ignore the small mud path going to your right.

14.37 **Continue up the hill slightly to your left, signposted 'Kuk Po via Shek Nga Tau'.** Ignore the path to the right signposted 'Kuk Po'.

15.43 **At the top of the hill turn right.** You will walk downhill along the main path. Ignore the narrow, treacherous path to your left.

15.78 **Turn right at the junction, taking the wide mud path down the hill and ignoring all other paths.** Ignore any smaller paths which branch off to the left or right. You pass a signpost labelled 'Kuk Po' after about 760m and walk through the old tiered village fields about 80m after this signpost. Continue through the fields in the same general direction until you reach the concrete path. The mud path you are on may split into several small paths which all head in the same general direction, you can take any one of these.

16.69 **Turn right at the concrete path.** Continue along this main path, ignoring any other concrete paths or stairs which may lead down towards your left.

16.79 ****ATTENTION**** Turn sharp left at the junction between concrete paths near the lamp post and telephone post, (**Figure 5**). Ignore the concrete path to your right. You should now be walking with the village on your left and the coast on your right. If not, it's the wrong direction.

Figure 5: Turn left along the concrete path at the junction.

17.09 **Turn right at the junction,** still along a concrete path. Ignore the concrete path to your left leading to more of the village.

Continue along the main concrete path. Ignore side paths leading to groups of village houses on your left. Your path will ultimately bend around to the right.

17.64 **Turn left when you reach the coast** and continue along the concrete path. There is a **toilet** here.

Continue along the concrete path which follows the coast.

19.10 **Follow the main path around to the right,** continuing along the coast. Ignore the path to your left which leads to 'Fung Hang Village'. Your path bends around in an 'S' shape before arriving at some concrete stairs.

19.23 **Climb the concrete stairs.** You will pass through a barbecue site at the top of the hill before soon heading downhill again.

19.63 **Continue straight ahead** at the junction with the emergency helpline, ignoring the path sharply to your left which you took earlier in the day.

20.09 Continue along the wide concrete road you are on. Ignore the small path to your left heading into the village.

20.22 **Turn right** along the wide, tarmaced 'Bride's Pool Road'.

FOOD At the end of Bride's Pool Road, Luk Keng is on your left. There is food available here if you are hungry.

20.50 ****FINISH****

GETTING HOME Take green mini bus 56K (HK$7) or a taxi (about HK$90) to Fanling KCR station.

HIKE 10: Pak Tam Chung to Wong Shek via Sharp Peak

summary:

22.77km | 9h | Sai Kung & Clear Water Bay

starting point: 北潭涌

Pak Tam Chung

getting to start: from Sai Kung: or 9 or or $65 or *

✱96R Sundays & holidays only. This bus runs from Choi Hung MTR & Sai Kung.

Go to Sai Kung. Take green mini bus 7 (HK$10) or 9 (HK$5.5) or bus 94 (HK$5.5) or bus 96R, (Sundays and holidays only, HK$15.6) or a taxi (about HK$65) to Pak Tam Chung, which is not the terminus for any of these buses, so please ask where to get off. (More info. on getting to Sai Kung, Appendix, A-iii).

description:

The hike starts at Pak Tam Chung and passes Tsak Yue Wo where a hidden path takes us to Tai Cham Koi. An undulating route leads to Tai Mun Shan before heading to Tai Wan beach. The path passes Tung Wan beach then climbs up to Sharp Peak. Now it's generally down hill to Wong Shek Pier.

getting home: 94 or $90 or 96R * to Sai Kung

✱96R Sundays & holidays only. This bus runs to Sai Kung & Choi Hung MTR.

Take bus 94 or a taxi (about HK$100) from Wong Shek to Sai Kung. On weekends and holidays bus 96R runs to Sai Kung and then on to Choi Hung MTR. There's an infrequent ferry from Wong Shek to Ma Liu Shui, which is close to University KCR station. (See main text).

WARNINGS:

A hard technical hike. Tai Mun Shan is extremely steep and overgrown. The path comes close to some steep, dangerous cliffs and passes along a ridge on its way to Sharp Peak. Not recommended for anyone with a fear of heights. The descent from Sharp Peak is incredibly steep, slippery and technical.

hike Xsection:

km from start	

GETTING TO START Go to Sai Kung and take green mini bus 7 or 9 or bus 94 (every day) or 96R (Sundays and holidays only) or a green taxi (about HK$65) to Pak Tam Chung.

START

With your back to the road, walk past the 'Sai Kung Country Park Visitor Centre' on your right and continue straight ahead, directly away from the road. You pass some toilets on your right hand side.

0.12 **Continue to the back right hand corner of the car park. Pass under the large arch labelled 'Pak Tam Chung', (Figure 1).** This also has 'Barbecue Site' and 'Family Walk' written on it.

Figure 1: Pass through the arch labelled 'Pak Tam Chung'.

0.23 **Turn left,** passing the toilet on your right hand side. Ignore the path up to the barbecue site and the steep concrete path going up towards your left.

0.78 **Continue straight ahead, signposted 'Tsak Yue Wu'.** Ignore the path going up to your left signposted 'Tai Mong Tsai Road'.

0.85 Follow the family walk around to the right, ignoring the narrow mud path leading straight ahead.

1.20 **Continue straight ahead, signposted 'Tsak Yue Wu',** ignoring the path to your left signposted 'Pak Tam' and 'Yung Shue O'.

1.35 **Continue straight ahead slightly to the left at the village houses,** along the concrete path. Ignore the concrete path to your right.

1.49 **Turn left at the large road.**

1.62 ****ATTENTION**** **STOP when you reach the box-like, light blue pumping station on your left, about 130m after turning onto the road. Cross the road and climb the concrete stairs directly ahead you, which begin just before the concrete slope, (Figure 2).**

Follow the narrow concrete slope upwards towards the left. This may not seem like a real path.

1.66 **Turn right onto the small mud path** after climbing the slope for about 40m.

1.90 Continue straight ahead, ignoring the small path to your left.

2.86 **Continue straight ahead,** ignoring the path going down the hill to your right. 10m later there is a small fork in the path, but both these minor paths soon rejoin each other.

Figure 2: Climb the concrete stairs and follow the slope up towards the left.

3.85 **Turn left, continuing up the hill.** Ignore the wider path which continues straight ahead towards the right.

4.04 ****TRIG. STATION** On Tai Cham Koi turn right down the mud path which begins about 7m BEFORE you reach the trigonometrical station.**

Follow the path as it bends around to the left after about 20m.

4.22 **Turn left** at the junction with the clear mud path.

4.87 **Turn right** at the junction with the clear, wide mud path. Ignore the path to your left and the path straight ahead up the hill. After about 70m you will pass distance post C5306.

Continue along the main trail, ignoring various smaller paths which lead to campsites.

5.80 **Continue straight ahead slightly to the left.** Ignore the wide mud path to the right.

6.33 **Turn sharp left, signposted 'Chek Keng',** at the junction at the bottom of the stairs. Ignore the path to the right, signposted 'Sai Wan'.

7.54 Cross the small stream at the bottom of the hill, continuing along your path. You will cross another small stream after about 180m.

8.06 ****ATTENTION** Turn right up the steep, overgrown mud path which begins just as your path crosses a large, pinkish, flat, rocky surface, (Figure 3). From the position where you turn right you can just about see a wide stream at the bottom of the hill**

about 150m ahead of you. DO NOT continue along the main path down to this stream. If you reach the stream, you have missed the path.

Figure 3: Turn right up the overgrown path at the large rocky surface.

Continue straight ahead up the steep, overgrown path. Ignore smaller paths to your left or right. In general you will climb for about 1.01km, then bend around to the left as the path heads towards the peak of Tai Mun Shan. You may need to push your way through some thick undergrowth in order to follow the path but it always remains visible and possible to follow.

9.44 ****TRIG. STATION**** On Tai Mun Shan, pass the trigonometrical station on your right and take the path going down the hill ahead of you slightly towards the left, (Figure 4). Ignore the path leading sharply to your left as well as that to your right.

Figure 4: Follow the path down the hill after passing the trigonometrical station.

9.55 Follow the steep, slippery main path around to the right, ignoring the smaller path to your left. The path will generally continue down the hill.

10.23 **Turn right at the concrete path.** You are now on the MacLehose trail and will be going downhill.

11.19 **At 'Tai Long Village' continue straight ahead, passing the restaurant on your left.** Ignore the two concrete paths to your right, the second of which you pass after about 30m. DO NOT continue along the MacLehose trail.

11.23 **Continue straight ahead,** crossing the small stream.

11.27 **Turn right,** following the clear but narrow concrete path signposted 'Tai Wan' on a makeshift signpost. The path soon becomes a mud path and passes some old village houses after about 290m.

11.88 **Continue straight ahead towards the sea once the path exits the woodland.** Ignore any paths to your left or right.

12.20 **Turn left at the beach.** You will be walking with the sea to your right.

12.53 ****ATTENTION**** **At the end of the beach continue straight ahead, taking the path which climbs immediately, slightly towards the right, (Figure 5). This path is indicated by a white arrow on a stone covered in white Chinese characters.** Ignore the other path which also continues in the same direction but does not immediately climb.

Figure 5: Continue along the path indicated by the white arrow.

12.65 ****WARNING** After about 120m you emerge at an open clearing near some cliffs. DO NOT take any of the paths which continue straight ahead slightly to the right. One of these paths comes within inches of a huge drop down a cliff. Please heed this warning.**

12.65 ****ATTENTION** At the small clearing near the cliffs follow the path to the left, around the small hill, (Figure 6). DO NOT continue straight ahead.**

12.70 **Turn right** at the junction with the narrow mud path. A pipe soon begins to run alongside your path.

Figure 6: Follow the path to the left around the small hill.

12.73 Continue straight ahead, following the pipe. Ignore any paths leading up or down the hill at any small junctions you may encounter.

ATTENTION After following the pipe for about 100m, please join the widest path running parallel to yours, in the same direction, about 4m down the hill. Just make sure you are beyond any cliffs before you do this. This path will eventually start to bend upwards and slightly to the left.

13.02 **Continue to the top of the small hill towards your left.** Ignore any much smaller paths going down towards the coast.

Once over the crest of the hill follow the path down towards the right.

13.17 ****ATTENTION**** **Cross the stream and take the path furthest towards the right which climbs the opposite bank, (Figure 7).** Ignore any smaller, less clear paths climbing the bank to your left.

13.18 **Turn sharp left immediately at the top of the bank,** along the narrow mud path.

Figure 7: Take the path up the bank furthest to your right

ATTENTION **Some of the small paths now described are a little unclear and you may need to improvise a bit to get to the large clear path that climbs Mai Fan Teng en route to Sharp Peak.**

13.20 **After about 20m continue straight ahead up the small tiered hill,** ignoring the path to your left.

13.22 **After about 20m continue up the hill towards your right.** Follow the path as it bends around to the left and continues climbing the small tiered fields.

13.24 **After about 20m follow the clear mud path towards your left.**

13.28 **Cross the small stream,** continuing up the hill along the clear mud path.

13.31 You should now be beginning to climb the clear, steep, muddy path up to Mai Fan Teng.

13.98 **Continue towards the left, up the hill along the main path.** Ignore the path down to your right.

Continue along the main path, ignoring any smaller paths going down to your left or right. The main path climbs over all the small hills you encounter, it does not go around them.

15.20 **Continue straight ahead, slightly to the right.** You are now beginning the final ascent to Sharp Peak. Ignore the path going down the hill to your left.

WARNING The path going down from the top of Sharp Peak is extremely steep, slippery and precarious. Please be extremely cautious.

15.44 ****TRIG. STATION** On Sharp Peak, pass the trigonometrical station and take the path slightly to your left,** which goes steeply down the hill.

15.68 **Turn right,** continuing along the main path. Ignore the path climbing the small hill directly ahead of you.

15.91 **Turn right,** continuing down the hill along the main path, ignoring the path to your left.

16.50 **Continue straight ahead up the hill** at the bottom of the steep slope. Ignore the paths to your left and right.

17.34 **Turn right at the concrete path near the emergency helpline.** You are now on the MacLehose trail and will pass mileage post M040 after about 190m.

18.46 **Continue straight ahead** at mileage post M042, ignoring the path down to your right.

SHORT CUT If you feel tired and wish to end your hike now then you can take the stairs going down to your right at mileage post M042. Cross the bridge to your right and follow this path along the coast until you reach a pier. There is a ferry at 10.20a.m. and 4.40p.m. to Wong Shek Pier which is the end of this hike. The same ferry also passes by again at 10.45a.m. and 5.05p.m. and this time goes all the way to Ma Liu Shui, which is very close to University KCR station. This trip takes about 2 hours but has some wonderful scenery. On weekends it is possible to take a small motor boat to Wong Shek

The ferry from to Ma Liu Shui offers some time to relax and amazing views.

Pier. You need to bargain your own price, but try not to pay more than about HK$20 per person. Catching a motor boat may also be possible on weekdays but the service is not so predictable or reliable.

18.80 Continue straight ahead, signposted 'Pak Tam Au' at the junction with the **emergency helpline.** Ignore the path to your right.

19.15 Continue along the main concrete path through the village. Ignore any paths branching off. The path bends a bit but continues in the same general direction.

19.31 Continue straight ahead slightly towards the right. Ignore the path towards the left heading towards some village houses.

19.90 You pass mileage post M045 on your right.

20.25 **ATTENTION** Continue straight ahead down the hill at the junction with the litter stockade, lamp post, youth hostel signpost and normal signpost. Your path is not signposted and immediately bends around to the left. **DO NOT** continue along the wide concrete MacLehose trail, signposted 'Pak Tam Au' or along the very narrow path straight ahead of you.

20.99 Turn right at To Kwa Peng village, down the hill along the concrete path. Ignore the path going straight ahead past the houses.

21.07 Turn left along the concrete path at the coast. You pass a small pier on your right after about 90m.

21.48 Turn right, signposted 'Wong Shek Pier'. Ignore the path continuing straight ahead up the hill.

21.74 Turn right, signposted 'Wong Shek Pier', on the wide mud path.

21.80 Turn right once again, signposted 'Wong Shek Pier'.

22.18 Continue along the main path. Ignore the steps to your left.

22.67 Turn sharply right, signposted 'Wong Shek Pier', walking down the stairs. Ignore the path straight ahead to your left signposted 'Wong Shek Tree Walk'.

22.77 **FINISH**

GETTING HOME Take bus 94 (every day) or 96R (Sundays & holidays only) or a taxi (about HK$100) from Wong Shek Pier to Sai Kung. There is also a ferry from Wong Shek to Ma Liu Shui, near University KCR. This ferry leaves at 10.35 and 16.55.

The descent from Sharp Peak is difficult, slippery but ultimately rewarding, hike 10.

Tai Long Wan, hike 10, at 7 in the morning - you'll have to start the hike early to get this view!

Just part of the vast repose of indifferent nature – as Turgenev would say.

APPENDIX

1. MTR & KCR map

Legend:

Station — Interchange ○

- Tsuen Wan Line
- Island Line
- Kwun Tong Line
- Tseung Kwan O Line
- Tung Chung Line
- Airport Express
- KCR West Rail
- KCR East Rail
- Ma On Shan Rail

Stations:

Wu Kai Sha, Ma On Shan, Heng On, Tai Shui Hang, Shek Mun, City One, Sha Tin Wai, Che Kung Temple, Tai Wai, Sha Tin, Fo Tan, University, Tai Po Market, Tai Wo, Fanling, Sheung Shui, Lo Wu

Tsuen Wan West, Kam Sheung Road, Yuen Long, Long Ping, Tin Shui Wai, Siu Hong, Tuen Mun

Tsuen Wan, Tai Wo Hau, Kwai Hing, Kwai Fong, Lai King, Mei Foo, Lai Chi Kok, Cheung Sha Wan, Sham Shui Po, Shek Kip Mei

Kowloon Tong, Lok Fu, Wong Tai Sin, Diamond Hill, Choi Hung, Kowloon Bay, Ngau Tau Kok, Kwun Tong, Lam Tin, Yau Tong

Po Lam, Hang Hau, Tseung Kwan O, Tiu Keng Leng

Tsim Sha Tsui East, Hung Hom, Mong Kok, Yau Ma Tei, Prince Edward, Nam Cheong, Tsim Tsa Tsui, Jordan

Olympic, Kowloon, Hong Kong, Tsing Yi, Airport, Tung Chung

Central, Admiralty, Wan Chai, Causeway Bay, Tin Hau, Fortress Hill, North Point, Quarry Bay, Tai Koo, Sai Wan Ho, Shau Kei Wan, Heng Fa Chuen, Chai Wan, Sheung Wan

2. Bus routes used in this book

bus	departs from	arrives at	departure times mon. - fri.	sat.	sun. & hols.	HK$
7	Sai Kung Terminus	Hoi Ha Village	8.15 - 18.15 every 30 min.		8.15 - 18.15 every 20 min.	10
7	Hoi Ha Village	Sai Kung Terminus	8.45 - 18.45 every 30 min.		8.45 - 18.45 every 20 min.	10
9	Sai Kung terminus	Lady MacLehose holiday village	6.30 - 20.30 every 30 min.		7.00 - 21.00 every 30 min.	5.5
20C	Tai Po Market	Tai Mei Tuk	5.30 - 1.00a.m. every 6-10 min.			6
20C	Tai Mei Tuk	Tai Po Market	6.00 - 1.30a.m. every 6-10 min.			6
56K	Fanling	Luk Keng	6.00 - 19.30 every 10-30 min.			7
56K	Luk Keng	Fanling	6.30 - 20.10 every 10-30 min.			7
64K	Tai Po Market	Yuen Long (West)	5.40 - 00.10 every 5-15 min.			6.9
65A	Shatin Central	Wong Nai Tau	9.00 - 23.20 every 5 min.			3.7
65A	Wong Nai Tau	Shatin Central	9.00 - 23.20 every 5 min.			3.7
69K	Sui Wo Road	Shatin	6.30 - 23.45 every 4-10 min.			5.2
75K	Tai Po Market	Tai Mei Tuk	6.05 - 24.00 every 9-20 min.			4.7
75K	Tai Mei Tuk	Tai Po Market	5.30 - 23.35 every 6-10 min.			4.7
82	Shing Mun reservoir	Tsuen Wan	5.50 - 23.30 every 10-30 min.			3.6
94	Sai Kung terminus	Wong Shek pier	6.00 - 21.00 every 30-35 min.		7.00 - 21.00 every 30 min.	5.5
94	Wong Shek pier	Sai Kung terminus	6.30 - 21.35 every 30-35 min.		7.30 - 21.35 every 30-35 min.	5.5
96R	Diamond Hill	Wong Shek pier	NO SERVICE	NO SERVICE	7.30 - 18.20 every 12-20 min.	15.6
96R	Wong Shek pier	Diamond Hill	NO SERVICE	NO SERVICE	8.40 - 19.30 every 12-20 min.	15.6

3. Extra transport directions for the hikes in this book

i. HIKE 1: Shatin to 65A

Go to Shatin KCR, take the exit which leads into the shopping plaza.

Walk straight through the plaza. After about 300m go down two flights of stairs and continue outside.

■ 350m

Once outside turn left, walking to the road.

■ 100m

Turn right at the road, walk about 50m to the 65A bus stop on the corner.

Go to Tai Po Market KCR, take the exit signposted bus terminus, where there is a subway straight ahead slightly to your left. Ignore the exit opposite the ticket office.

Walk down the subway for about 25m until you reach a junction.

25m   **25m**

Turn left at the junction.

5m

Turn right, climbing the stairs next to the toilet. The 20C bus stop is on your left.

64K + **75K**

Turn right, signposted 'Bus Terminus'. Ignore the stairs to your left after 20m. Your path bends to the left.

40m

Continue straight ahead, signposted '64K, 75K, 275R'. Ignore the path to your right, signposted 'KCR Feeder Bus'.

30m

Turn right, signposted '75K, 64K, 275R'

30m

Climb the stairs to the bus terminus. After 50m the 75K is left, the 64K right.

iii. HIKES 6 & 10: getting to Sai Kung

Go to Choi Hung MTR, take exit C2.

Walk up to the road.

150m

At the road, turn left and walk 20m to the bus stop for mini bus 1M.

Go to Fanling KCR.

Find the walkway signposted with the mini bus and taxi (this could be on your right or left, depending on which exit you took).

2m

Turn left, walk down the stairs. You reach the taxi rank after 30m, the 56k stop is to your right.

4. Useful numbers & contacts

i. Emergency numbers

General emergency	999
Fire control centre	2720 0777
Police crime hotline	2527 7177

ii. Taxi firms

Shatin & Fo Tan area	2697 4333
Tai Po & Tai Mei Tuk	2657 2267
Sai Kung area	2729 1199

iii. Public transport

Kowloon Motor Bus	2745 4466	www.kmb.com.hk
KCR	2602 7799	www.kcrc.com
MTR	2881 8888	www.mtr.com.hk
Transport department	2804 2600	www.info.gov.hk/td

iv. Weather

Hong Kong observatory	2926 8200	www.hko.gov.hk/contente.htm

v. Environmental

Agriculture, Fisheries and Conservation department	2708 8885	www.afcd.gov.hk/index_e.htm
Env. Protection Dept.	2835 1018	www.epd.gov.hk/epd
Friends of the Earth	2528 5588	www.foe.org.hk
WWF	2526 1011	www.wwf.org.hk
Greenpeace	2854 8300	www.greenpeace-china.org.hk

vi. Countryside Series map outlets

23/F North Point Gov.   2231 3187   18/F Harbour Building   2852 4216
Offices   38 Pier Road
333 Java Road   Central
North Point   Hong Kong Island
Hong Kong Island

382 Nathan Rd   2780 0981
Yau Ma Tei
Kowloon

vii. Hiking shops

Protrek   2332 8699   Protrek   2529 6988
466-472 Nathan Road   46 Hennessy Road
Yau Ma Tei   Wan Chai
Kowloon   Hong Kong Island

World Sports Co. Ltd. 2396 9357   Glory Sporting Eqpt.   2380 6261
1/F, 83 Fa Yuen Street   1/F 198 Sai Yeung Choi
Mong Kok   Sreet
Kowloon   Mong Kok
                                   Kowloon

viii. Trailwalking and trailrunning events

Trailwalker   www.oxfamtrailwalker.org.hk

King of the Hills   www.seyonasia.com/competitions.html

Green Power HK Trail   www.greenpower.org.hk

Phoenix walkathon   www.travel.to/pworghk

Raleigh marathon   www.raleigh.org.hk/rimm

The Sowers Action   www.sowers.org.hk

Action Asia Adventure Races   www.actionasia.com/aae

for hiking or trekking ……

HK**HIKING.COM**

HAPPY • HIKING • HAPPY • HIKERS

CATBUS ADVENTURES

HIKING • TREKKING • OVERSEAS ADVENTURES
www.catbus-adventures.com